*"The afterlife has obsessed
walked upright. We are all (
where we're going when it's all over—and we crave detailed
dispatches from the other side. In T. Marie Bell's thoroughly
detailed and fascinating story of her near-death experience,
we have one of the most compelling accounts of the after-life I
have ever read. This book will answer questions you probably
didn't even know that you had, and do it in a moving and
uplifting narrative that will stay with you long after you read
the final page."*

**-Nick Chiles
Pulitzer Prize-winning journalist and
New York Times best selling author:**

Every Little Step - My Story: Bobby Brown

The Rejected Stone: Al Sharpton and the Path to America Leadership

The Blueprint: A Plan for Living Above Life's Storms with Kirk Franklin

I HEARD GOD'S VOICE

How I Died, Came Face-to-Face
with God, and Lived to tell the Story

T. Marie Bell

Success Write Now

For information about special discounts for bulk purchase please contact
Success Write Now at: info@successwritenow.com

Unless otherwise noted, Scripture quotations are taken from the King James
Version of the Bible (KJV).

Scripture quotations noted NIV are taken from the Holy Bible, New
International Version (NIV). Copyright 1973, 1978, 1984 by International Bible
Society. Used by permission of Zondervan Publishing House. All rights
reserved.

Printed in the United States of America
Library of Congress Control Number: 2020908582
ISBN: 978-1-7334053-0-0
Ebook ISBN: 978-1-7334053-1-7

*This book is based on the author's recollection of true events that transpired
during a near-death experience. Some names and identifying characteristics
have been changed to protect the privacy of those depicted.*

I dedicate this book to my daughter, Sierra. Without you, this book would not have been possible.

I dedicate this book to my unborn child. It is because of you this book has been brought to life. May you rest in peace.

"With man this is impossible, but with God all things are possible."
(Matthew 19:26, NIV)

ACKNOWLEDGMENTS

I must first thank God for blessing me on this journey called life. By the power of a second chance, I am able to share my testimony with the world to display God's love and abounding grace. I pray my sincere effort in telling this story pleases you and will bless many.

Howard Fike, my deceased grandfather, this heartfelt thank you is given in loving memory of your sweet spirit and unconditional love that molded me into the woman that I am today. Thank you for your steadfast encouragement. I love you so much. Papa, you are deeply missed.

Derrick Adkins, Olympic Gold Medalist, and trusted friend. Your sound counsel was priceless in supporting me with this book. Thank you for that motivational push that jumpstarted this project.

Nick Chiles, 3x New York Times best-selling author, I extend a huge thank you for the gracious things you said in the endorsement of my book. I cannot thank you enough.

Anthony "AJ" Joiner, author, strategist, and consultant, I graciously thank you for your professional advice. You truly challenged me to step out and execute my vision valiantly. I so needed that. Thank you immensely.

Shashonna Smith, coder, editor, and longtime childhood friend, thank you for leaping in at the 11th hour to give a listening ear and critical eye to my project. Your advice was invaluable. I appreciate you so very much for your assistance.

To my daughter, Sierra, God blessed me richly with you. You are my little angel on earth. I am thankful for the covenant that I made to God when I discovered that I was pregnant. The blessings received were due to that covenant. I love you tremendously and can't wait to see what God has in store for your life. It's going to be huge!

To my mother, father, and siblings, Kita and Justin, thank you for your love and support. I love you more than you will ever know. You guys mean the world to me. Mom, thank you so very much for all of the sacrifices that you made when I was younger to ensure that my siblings and I had everything that we needed and never wanted for anything. I love you.

Dorothy Winbush Riley, a.k.a. Ma Riley, author, and friend, I will always remember our conversation right before your untimely passing from ovarian cancer. I asked what motivated you to write? You took a deep breath and said, "You have to search deep within your spirit to find your voice. You have to ask yourself what powerful message do you want to share with the world?" Your words are forever ingrained in my heart. Thank you for your wisdom. I found that voice and I am shouting my message loud and clear.

Last but not least, to Dia Parrish, I give a heartfelt, humble, and grateful thank you. I am thankful to God for placing you in my life at just the right time. Thank you for being by my side when I needed you most. You are such an amazing person and the true definition of a lifesaver. Words cannot express my gratitude and how much you mean to me. I love you from the bottom of my heart and thank you until my last breath for everything.

CONTENTS

PROLOGUE

E veryone has a journey and a story to tell. Mine is profound. I literally died, gripped the clutches of death, was resuscitated back to life, and virtually told no one about this experience out of fear, shock, and shame. Many of my family members will discover the remnants that unraveled that night for the first time just like you. It will happen as randomly as the lady who purchased this book online and curled up on a chaise in Los Angeles. Or, as sporadically as the teenager who opened the cover to read on a crowded bus in Chicago. It's a testimony that I've virtually shared with no one. I've struggled for years trying to understand why God allowed this to happen? Why am I still alive? What did he want me to do? I wasn't sure. But at the same time, I wasn't ready to reveal the facts leading up to that night either. The truth of the matter is I was no angel. Yet, I had a tendency to walk around with embellished wings to create the image of perfection as if I were. In sharing my experience, it would equally entail exposing my past and the mistakes that I made. Which like most, I would rather forget and tiptoe to focus on my accomplishments instead. But, God doesn't work that way. He wants you to humble yourself and acknowledge your faults. He wants you to reveal through a powerful testimony how you made it through. It's not easy and you have to be transparent. I was never quite ready to expose such intimate elements of myself considering I'm typically so private. I rarely share anything with anyone unless I trust you. And, I trust no one. So unless I've known you for at least 10 years, the likelihood of you being let into my world is next to Neveruary. Even then, the reality of knowing me 100% will be circumvented. I battled for years holding onto this event that led to me hearing the voice of God. Until finally, I realized my purpose is to share this experience with the world. My destiny is to reach that person who needs to hear this testimony and speak a word to that individual who constantly questions his or her faith. So I will disclose my skeletons in order to touch that young teen or college girl who may have fallen peril to temptation, done some shameful things, and wonders if God forgives her? To offer hope to that single mother who's done everything alone for years, downtrodden, frustrated, and wondering when her breakthrough will come? It is my desire for everyone holding this book right now to realize that I, just like you, was also at a crossroads in my life. I made the best decision I knew at the time. One that nearly cost me my life yet formed the deepest relationship I now have with God. An experience that only one percent of the population will ever have: to actually hear the voice of God. So as I begin, understand this is a difficult stage to stand on and a very challenging microphone to grab. Yet, I finally mustered the courage to come forward and expose myself to you, who may be struggling with your life, your purpose, and your existence. God is still in the miracle-making business.

He is capable of doing incredible things in spite of all of the chaos going on around you. In the same way that God spoke to me and miraculously altered my life for the better, he can do the same for you. I pray that you are given clarity and a fresh trajectory as you immerse in my experience. Trust me, it's pretty intense.

I know you are wondering where and how it all began. My story is complex and heavily layered. But, when you peel the layers back, it actually spiraled out of control and unfolded just like this...

BLACK OUT

I awoke abruptly out of my sleep. I didn't realize I was knocked out for hours. Like a typical summer night in Atlanta, my dorm room was dark, muggy, and still. I saw my college roommate, Lil D, resting peacefully on the other side of the room in her small twin bed. She looked so serene. I wish I could say the same. My body felt like it was hit by a freight train. My stomach twisted in pain, the same as it had hours earlier on the football field. Only, this time worse! My mouth became increasingly dry. Sweat trickled down my forehead. My eyes hysterically darted to and fro. Only instants remained before I would hurl in the worst kind of way *oh no here it comes! Where's the trashcan?* I thought. Pain shot down my side. I tried to raise myself out of bed. But, the pain was too severe. A textbook fell from the foot of the bed with a loud thump waking Lil D. I continued to anxiously search in the dark. I had to find it and fast!

"You, ok?!" A quizzical Lil D sat upright in her bed staring at me intently.

"No! I gotta throw up!" I wailed.

Where's the freaking trashcan?! I panicked. I searched and searched. In the nick of time, I found it stashed right behind my bed. Like a volcano about to erupt, I shot forth all the contents weighing in on my belly. But, nothing much came up except thick liquidity mucus. I sat back on the bed heaving again. More vomit erupted. Instead of feeling better, I felt worse! The sharp aches were excruciating. It felt as if King Kong towered above me and delivered blow after blow of massive non-stop upper-cuts to the gut.

"Tee! Tee!!" Lil D screamed.

I stared blankly back. As much as I wanted to respond, I couldn't. I opened my parched mouth. But no words came out. I leaned against the bed. I tilted my head towards the ceiling. I blacked out.

Now, this didn't just occur out the blue. Nor, was this everything that happened on that traumatic night either. Trust me, things got much worse. There are always consequences to bear for every action that you make. And, my immoral decisions finally caught up with me. But, before I get ahead of myself. It's not fair to give you just a glimpse of that fateful night. It's important that you get the full story. To do that, you have to go back, way back. Let me take you to the very beginning. But, be forewarned. My story starts in one of the coldest, one of the most violent, and one of the most economically oppressed environments that you can imagine. Yes, my story begins in the heart of Detroit most notably known as "the D".

IT'S SO COLD IN THE D

I grew up in a single-parent home on the northwest side of Detroit. It seemed my mother was the only single mother on the block for the longest time. Of course, it didn't start off that way. My parents wed directly out of high school like many young teens during that time. Back then things were different. If a young girl became pregnant, it didn't matter how long the couple dated. No one cared how well the families got along. Or, the fact the pregnancy might have been a mistake. No sir! You got married. Period. And, that's exactly what my parents did.

My father was a handsome young man with a striking midnight complexion, wide smile, and confident swagger to match. He worked extended hours at General Motors during the day and was one of the coolest keyboardists in a local band by night. My mother was a revolutionary type woman with an Angela Davis Afro, sunshine skin, and a petite curvaceous frame. Instead of attending Spelman College as originally planned, she found herself pushing long hours at the United States Post Office after getting knocked up directly after graduation, and popping out my sister, Kita shortly thereafter. Needless to say, I quickly followed behind on her heels.

Given the lay of the land, things went relatively well aside from my dad's numerous flirtatious romps at his nightly gig. My mother was a tiny firecracker of a woman and his disrespectful antics created a trickle-down dichotomy of negative tidings to come. One night, a heated argument erupted in our small kitchen as my mom's determine talk of divorce became the lone freedom cry that led to one of the worst beatings she endured. Crimson droplets dripped from my father's fist and blood gushed from my mother's lacerated eye. This chain of events became many coupled with my mom drawing a gun and attempting to kill my dad. I shook with fear in the corner wall as my big sister hugged me close. Articles of our home were broken, blood was splattered across the carpet, and the police arrived in the nick of time. Welcome to the D and welcome to my life at the tender age of four. I observed violence and survival at a very premature age. I witnessed even more betrayal and broken trust thereafter. This city gripped the weary with a treacherous grasp. There was little room for error and no mercy for the innocent. Living within the confines of Detroit you had to be on your P's and Q's at all times. This was a city of violence. This was a city of scandal. This was the same city before child abduction became fashionable; I was almost kidnapped by a family friend at the tender age of 10. Yes, it's so true and it's so cold in the D.

M y street, like all others on Detroit's west side, looked pristine for a lower-middle-class neighborhood. Ours was a block lined with modest two-story brick houses, towering trees, and uniform globe lights on the front lawn bearing each home's address. A neighborhood where residents lived for 15 plus years, kids were about the same age, and no one ever intended to leave. People took pride in their families, their lawns, their homes, and their cars. But, don't get it twisted. Detroit was notable for having "pockets of elements" in every neighborhood. The real story that swept through all the manicured lawns, where children cautiously played, and neighbors stopped at the end of the walk for friendly banter told a different story. One that was hard to see on the outside looking in. My block was no different. It seemed almost every other summer we became a little too familiar with the S.W.A.T. team raids from doors being kicked in across the street, to eight houses down searching for my best friend's father, a prison escapee, to right next-door looking for the next up and rising kingpin. This was Prest Street, where kids truly matriculated through the school of hard knocks. If you survived past your senior year, it seemed your only career path was that of a teacher, a police officer, a factory worker, or a drug dealer. And somehow all were equally respected professions.

Given this environment, you can only imagine how hard it must've been for my mother to raise two girls within these elements. She did all she could to keep my sister and me in church and in the best magnet schools in the city. My grandfather, a sweet man with kind eyes, quiet nature, and a humble spirit, picked up the slack where he could. Working tirelessly and faithfully as a janitor for over 25 years in the

Detroit Public School system, he saved his hard-earned money to pour hundreds of dollars into my piano lessons from ages six to sixteen to expose me to the classics, something different, something cultural, something most in my family didn't have. But, I didn't want to be a goody-two-shoes. I wanted to be cool. Being the leader of the pack is what made you stand out in my neighborhood. As long as you had respect, loyalty, and heart, you were considered in. Now true enough, I appreciated the balance my mother and grandfather brought trying to educate us. But, the reality is this exposure formulated an equation of a double threat with book smarts and street smarts. While many parents try to shelter their children from falling peril to the dark forces of the inner city, what they failed to realize was there's no escaping the streets as a teen living in Detroit. Especially if you didn't want to get ostracized, bullied, alienated, or worse yet, shot for being weak.

My sister, Kita, and I attended Cass Technical High School located in downtown Detroit. We woke at the crack of dawn every single day to catch three city buses to get there. Cass Tech was one of the most prestigious high schools in the city. Many of the greats including singer Diana Ross, actress Lily Tomlin, automobile executive John De Loreon, Miss USA Kenya Moore, comedian David Allen Grier and a host of others set the precedent of sophistication there as well. Cass Tech was set apart for the gifted and only allowed students who tested in above a B average to attend. But, the dynamic here is while we received the best education the city had to offer, one critical problem still remained. Once the school day drew to a close we had to return home. We had to morph into chameleons in order to switch gears, survive, and thrive in our community. We kicked it with our neighborhood friends, the around the way kids who went to Cooley High. Although we didn't attend Cooley, it goes without saying that the majority of the guys that we dated in and around our neighborhood did. These were the same guys who ran with the Puritan Avenue Boys and Y.B.I. The same boys who sold drugs, drove flashy cars, and looked out for you through lavish means of shoes, jewelry, and gear. These material trinkets were the things that mattered to teens in my neighborhood. Sure I was taught in school about the endless possibilities of wealth achieved through working in bountiful industries. But, I didn't see it. The primary industries that ran Detroit were the automobile industry and the drug industry. And most people's families were involved in both. So while the school system educated us, the possibilities and ethics taught through the mantra of hard work to attain financial success seemed as realistic as having Sunday tea with the Easter Bunny. I didn't know anyone making that kind of living. In my neighborhood your options were limited. You could date a guy in school with a mall job or date a guy from the neighborhood with a street job. After high school, you could date a guy who worked for the auto plant. Or, date a drug dealer who controlled the streets. In the end, they both would marry you and they both went to church.

I was raised in a black Baptist church that I attended religiously. Surprisingly, a lot of doughboys from around my neighborhood went as well. It's actually an interesting dynamic when you think of the violence that envelops the city coupled with the number of people who attend church regularly. But unlike everyone else, although I went to church frequently, I constantly rebelled against it. As a matter of fact, my mother would actually force me to go every Sunday. I remember many beat downs erupting from shoes being thrown at my head to belt whips across my back simply because I didn't want to attend. This episode of events became a steadfast Sunday ritual that occurred like clockwork every week in my home. From the minute the alarm clock sounded and the loud gospel music wailed the conversation pretty much went the same.

"Get up and get ready for church!" My mother yelled up the stairs.

"I don't feel like it!" I shouted back.

"You better get downstairs and in this bathroom!"

Her voice elevated two octaves. "Don't make me come upstairs!"

I slowly shuffled down the staircase holding onto the banister and giving serious face.

"Why do I have to go?!" I wailed.

"Because I said so!"

"You're always trying to make somebody do
something they don't want to do!" I stormed past her.

Crack! Smacks upside the back of my head followed. Luckily, my sister was smart enough to just stay quiet, get dressed, and comply. Kita had a cool around-the-way-girl persona with honey brown skin and a cute curvaceous figure. She wanted no problems with my mother. She'd rush in the bathroom and swiftly put herself together. However, the rebel in me would hear nothing of it. My mantra was, I lived in a free country. And, if I didn't want to go to church, I shouldn't have to go. That was simple enough right? Well, apparently not if you lived in my mother's home. She made it very clear that her household was not a democracy and the almighty black leather belt backed up her bill of rights.

So there I found myself sitting in the sanctuary every week front and center for Sunday school, singing in the church choir, and seething on the inside from it all. I resented church and I resented my mother as well. In the whole scheme of things, I wanted to know what good was church going to do. Why did God let bad things happen to good people? Why couldn't my mom get a boyfriend or a break after her divorce? Why wasn't my life better? I witnessed all the brat pack kids at Cass Tech living it up. Their parents had handsome salaries, fancy titles, lavish cars, and homes in the best neighborhoods. Meanwhile, my mother was struggling to survive. Why did we always have to go to church and still nothing changed? I wondered why did God allow the car-jackings, drive-by shootings, teen deaths, drugs, and broken homes? It seemed this whole institution of religion was so hypocritical and I didn't want any part of it. But needless to say, I didn't have much choice in the matter. By the end of my freshman year of high school, I was a part of every youth group in the church and had a ton of friends. But, my sentiments remained the same. I only looked forward to kicking it with my crew. I didn't partake in the church activity, faith, and worship, to lead a closer walk with God. That wasn't about to happen. In fact, the exact opposite began to fester. I started to question whether there even was a God. I know. This was a pretty ironic stance for a person who sat in the holy sanctuary regularly. But, I stood my ground anyway.

I didn't understand God and I definitely didn't fear him. I didn't fear much of anything. I was rebellious. The more my mother tried to make me worship, the more I tried to prove you can drag me to church but you can't control my mind, my beliefs, or my actions. I truly started doubting God. And, in the rare moments of acknowledging that he *may* exist, I decided that God definitely didn't care about black people. African-Americans could never get a break. Everyone I knew was struggling and it seemed the struggling never ended. I couldn't wait to get out of this place. I couldn't wait to get away from my mother. Once I graduated high school, I couldn't wait to get out of the D.

TESTING MY LIMITS

High school in the '90s ruled! There were no gadgets to bring to school and you didn't have to worry about your friends constantly updating social media accounts. Friends had to talk face-to-face to share stories. And, when you didn't know something you had to actually read a book or figure it out. The one thing I quickly figured out was the fact that I needed freedom and lots of it! My high school experience was pretty much the same. I desperately licked my chops for a chance of freedom and attempted to break loose at any opportunity I saw fit. But, my options were limited and I was sheltered virgin up until 10th grade, albeit sheltered under a different pretense. My mother kept me in-line by bombarding my life with extra-curricular activities, church, and forcing me to constantly babysit my baby brother all in an effort to control the remainder of my teen life. My father was pretty much a lost cause even though I saw him every other weekend. He lackadaisically focused his parenting on benign things that didn't deal with the real world. My dad's primary focus was to have fun. And, he spared no cost from going to the arcade, movies, go-cart racing, and countless amusement parks. We had a ball! Hanging out with my dad was always a fun time. But, when it came to serious issues, my dad was like a tennis court without a net, useless. During my teen years, my father never spoke with me about drugs, dating, or sex. The pink elephant was always in the room and he would rather forget that the real world existed than confront any issue head-on. My mother was a step ahead of my dad and when she attempted to tackle "the talk", she gave the best advice that she could muster.

"You shouldn't have sex until you get married." She dryly breathed.

"Well, what if I never get married?" I sarcastically countered.

"Then, you shouldn't have sex with anyone unless you love them enough to have their baby."

Now, I have to admit. This was the single worst advice anyone could possibly give a teenage girl. As a teen, you're in love with someone new every week. I was no different. This lack of concrete guidance left me to my own instincts and those of my clueless friends. I had to utilize my surroundings to make the best decisions when it came to relationships, dating, and sexual interactions. Needless to say, this was my downfall.

My social life evolved during high school. Cass Tech was huge with 5000 students scattering through the halls like mice to reach eight floors in five minutes. The seniors were given the most privileges because they had paid their dues and were headed out the door anyway. Their lockers were situated on the first and second floors. Juniors were given the third and fourth floors. Sophomores had to hike it to the fifth and sixth floors. And freshman had to run to the seventh and eighth floors no matter where their next class existed. This was hell! So, I was ecstatic when my sister was gracious enough to let me, a lowly freshman, share a locker with her on the prestigious second floor. I was the only freshman amidst a sea of seniors during class changes. I ogled at all the tall, attractive, older guys on that floor while mentally taking note of the senior girls' swag, hair, and makeup to stash in my repertoire of replication. Now, while I was in a world of awe, there is always a downside to being out of your element. Being surrounded by 17 and 18-year-olds brought on a different kind of social exposure to a tender 14-year-old. My 411 came from two senior girls on the cheer team who regurgitated the same conversation every Friday. I would eagerly approach my locker, shuffle my sister's articles, stall, and listen. Then like clockwork, I'd hear the leader of the pack with her slender frame and spiral ponytail, smack her gum, play in her hair, look at her friend and squeal.

"Girl, it's Friday! Time to go see my man and do what I do best!"

"I know that's right!" Her sidekick snickered.

I remembered standing there like an idiot thinking: *What is she talking about? What does she do best?* It literally took me months before I figured out she was talking about sex. It sounded fun, interesting, and apparently made you super popular. I wanted to partake in sex too. But, there was just one problem. I was a serious late bloomer. I was well into the ninth grade still without my period. And while my sister sported D cups, my underdeveloped body only filled A's. I was pretty petite, standing just a few inches over 5 feet, and only weighed 95 pounds. The only thing I had working in my favor was a small waist, cute chocolate face, and asstronaumical butt. But still, I wouldn't be able to have fun and enjoy high school like the girls who bragged next to my sister's locker about their exciting and erotic Fridays.

That night, my mind was clouded. I sat at our small wooden dinner table with my mother and sister. Our kitchen was infused with an invisible cloud of welcoming scents of spices, butter, and delicious meat aromas. My mother promptly claimed her throne at the head of the table. My sister, a true replica of a B-girl from the Right On! teen magazine could care less about this nightly ritual. She grabbed her chair and plopped in it, as her oversized bangle earrings swayed against her fierce, long, asymmetrical bob. She fixated on the plate in front of her covered with mashed potatoes, meatloaf, and broccoli avoiding eye contact at all cost. She knew my mother was about to drill her on the school day and Kita wanted nothing more than to wolf down her food and escape this forced gathering. I, on the other hand, actually enjoyed our nightly dinners. It was family time, a period that my mother expected us to share and recap our day. It seemed my mother and I did most of the talking while my sister feigned interest. But, this particular night my mind raced. For some reason, I could not get that senior cheerleader out of my head or what she said. It wasn't like she discovered something new or broke the Da Vinci Code. But, her shrill laugh and innuendos still lingered. As silence fell over the table and the sound of munching replaced chitchat, I found myself zoning out.

"I think I'm really ready..." I vocalized in a trance-like state staring at my fork.

"Ready for what?" my Mom broke my daze.

"Huh?!" I hesitated.

"You just randomly said that you're ready." My mother's expression became intent.

"Yeah," I apprehensively shoved a spoonful of potatoes into my mouth.

"But, what did you mean?" My mom pressed again. "What are you ready for?"

My sister's eyeballs bulged. She reached for her glass and took a huge gulp. I didn't know what to do and I wasn't sure what to say. I couldn't believe I uttered something so absurd. There was no use in lying considering pervasive stutters would erupt anyway. So, I took a deep breath, laid my fork down, and put my big girl panties on.

"I think I'm ready to have sex." I blurted.

My sister spit her drink across the table and laughed hysterically. My mother gasped and clutched invisible pearls.

"What?!!"

"It's hard to explain." I picked up my fork. "I just think I am." I stuffed a forkful of potatoes in my mouth.

My sister continued laughing nonstop. Soda even shot from her nose.

"It's not even that funny!" I scolded.

"Yes, it is!" Kita wheezed.

My mother shook her head in disbelief. She stared at me evenly.

"Well, you know you can't have sex or you'll get pregnant." She coolly replied.

"No, I can't!" I defiantly shot back.

"Yes, you can." She smirked.

"How?!" My underdeveloped mind raced. "I don't even have my period yet."

"Well, that's how." My mom stated confidently.

"What?! That doesn't even make sense." I winced.

"Exactly!" She smiled. "You'll get pregnant because you never know when your period is coming."

My mother casually picked up her fork and continued eating already knowing the battle was won. *Curses!* That's when I got thrown in the biggest trick bag of them all. My mother hoodwinked me with my own lack of knowledge and tore up my sexual dream by turning it into a nightmare. What's more, she called every cousin and aunt from New York, to Ohio and from Alabama, to Louisiana to share the news of my self-proclaimed readiness. I was completely bummed, embarrassed, and still missing out on the fun Friday nights the senior girls talked about.

Sophomore year passed with the crimson tide finally coming. Junior year whizzed by with the experience of sexual conquests. And, I was living life full throttle, still religiously rebellious and full of anarchy toward parental control. I was a hellcat trying to get into everything imaginable. My friends and I were too smart for our own good. We helped one another figure out ways to sneak around, skip school, and basically stay in trouble without getting caught. By senior year, I craftily joined every activity at school so my mother wouldn't learn my real schedule. I became a member of the Cass Pep Club, the Drama Club, the Pommerettes, the Year Book Staff, and I was a Senior Rep to give the indication that I was always busy. Mom was just happy that I was staying out of trouble, or at least she thought. With my manipulative mind, I ensured I was always on the honor roll so that I could fly beneath the radar. Then, I'd skip school, leave early, or stay late to play hooky, of all places from home. I was becoming wild, reckless, and I didn't care. This was a dangerous way to live. In church, I heard many times that the Bible states in James 1:14-15 (KJV), "But every man is tempted, when he is drawn away of his own lust, and enticed. Then when lust hath conceived, it bringeth forth sin; and sin, when it is finished, bringeth forth death." At the time this meant nothing to me. After all, my mantra was, life is short. And as far as death is concerned, in Detroit, I'd do good to live past 25 years old anyway. Besides even if I did live longer, what kind of life would I have? Marry a man who worked for the plant and have four kids? Or marry a drug dealer, risk him being indicted, murdered, and left broke as a single mom? Given those were the only foreseeable odds, with neither being viable options, I just decided to live for the moment. I didn't really have a plan beyond going to college. My mother's primary concern was that I didn't get pregnant. She told me the start of senior year, "You have to go to college and it has to be out of state." Then she quickly added, "Oh, and you can't go to Ohio because that's too close." I didn't know what she meant at the time. And, I really didn't care. I was just doing me, having fun, and breaking all the rules.

IGNORING THE SPIRIT WITHIN

Senior year I was doing me to the fullest! But, it's amazing, no matter how foolish or unruly you are, even in those moments your spirit will guide, protect, and forewarn you. To the worldly, it's more commonly referred to as your conscience. But, to those spiritually inclined, it's called discernment of the Holy Spirit. It's that small voice within that speaks to you when your gut tells you something is wrong. It is God's subtle way of staying close and keeping your best interests at heart. It is written in Psalm 32:8 (KJV) "I will instruct thee and teach thee in the way which thou shalt go: I will guide thee with mine eye." But the problem with this guidance is that many of us choose to ignore the signs. I was no different. Looking back, I could see that God stayed very close to me. Even when I thought he didn't care. He began speaking his plan into my spirit very early. At first, it wasn't deliberate. Oftentimes, it would be a dream that would manifest itself in truth. But, I was too ignorant to appreciate the divine revelation that God so desperately wanted me to attain. I'd easily brush it off as déjà vu. Meanwhile, this inner voice was trying to warn me of impending danger. But, I was a Capricorn; stubborn, adamant, and self-righteous. I only wanted to do what I wanted to do and no more. For this reason, I would ignore all signs, signals, and gut intuition. Why would God speak to me? I didn't even want to worship him half the time. Whenever I heard of something phenomenal happening to someone, it was always a minister. Or some goody-two-shoes who didn't have a real struggle in the world. I never heard anyone's testimony where God outright spoke to a single mother, a promiscuous teen, a thief, an alcoholic, drug-addict, or someone struggling with real issues. So, I never really thought God would ever reach out to me. Especially when I renounced him every chance I got. But that's where we as human beings go wrong. We will never understand the full measure, omnipresence, or omnipotence of our heavenly father. We can never fathom who he chooses or why? I remembered hearing in church in Ephesians 2:8 (KJV), "For by grace are ye saved through faith; and that not of yourselves it is the gift of God." But, I was so lost at this point that I saw my sins as unforgivable. My faith was so shaky I was certain none of this could apply to me. But to the contrary, God reached out to me in a major way during my senior year. Even after all the partying, the boys, the sex, the disobedience, he still reached out. I will never forget the moment when I ignored his warning for the last time. I'll also never forget the person he tried to warn me about. He would be the reason for my demise, my fall, and my death.

AN ULTIMATE ADRENALINE RUSH

I was so excited when I first started working as a cashier at Foot Action USA. It was every teenage girl's dream to work at Northland Mall. I reveled in the new gig coupled with the fact that I was the only girl working in an all men's shoe store. The sales guys catered to my every whim and treated me like a princess. The entire staff was super young, carefree, spunky, and a total funhouse. Keith, the store manager, had an athletic build, towering presence, and dark ebony complexion. He was only 25 years old and the best boss in life. With all of this youthful energy, you can only imagine the enjoyable time that we had. Let's start with the cool idea to blare the latest bootleg movie on all four televisions smeared across the wall. Combined with the guys playing basketball, hockey, football, or whatever sports- related game they could invent while throwing socks and shoes around the premises. Yes, I admit. We were crazy teens and an HR nightmare. Luckily for us, there was no human resources department onsite. This was my dream job and I met so many cool guys in the Detroit area. Those hormone raging boys would ogle, flirt, and do whatever they could to catch my eye. I ate up all of this attention like a ravished cheetah and bragged to my friends about the attractive lot I entertained for the day. The numbers game quickly became an all-time favorite as I would tally the phone numbers I obtained at the end of the night. But, this game came to a quick halt the minute this one sexy specimen stepped through the door. When you envision a hot guy from the nineties, L.L. Cool J, Tupac, Nas, and a host of other B-boys fill the mental screen. This teen dream was no different. He was a complete hottie and encompassed all the physical attributes to match: warm mocha brown skin, curly black hair, and deep almond eyes. He was tall and slim with a distinct chiseled jawline. He strolled towards the register holding a box of Air Force Ones. As our eyes locked, his lips burst into a smile warm enough to melt a glacier. It was no wonder I stood behind the register whisked off, love at first sight.

"Welcome to Foot Action." I beamed. "You find everything ok?"

"Yeah, these are tight!" He flirtatiously smiled. "You new here?"

"How'd you know?" I grinned.

"I never saw a girl working the register before and I come here all the time."

I rang up his articles and tried to contain the massive butterflies fluttering in my stomach.

"Here you go." I handed him the bag and receipt.

"You got a boyfriend?"

"Huh?" I was totally caught off guard.

"Boyfriend," He questioned a second time.

"Umm no," I quickly regrouped.

"Then, why don't you give me your number?"

"I don't even know your name." I coyly grinned while attempting to throw a little swag into my groove.

"But, I know yours." He smiled.

"Oh yeah? Because I don't remember telling you." I playfully placed my hand on my hip.

"Tee right?"

"How'd you guess?" I stood perplexed.

" It's on your name tag." He pointed and laughed.

We both chuckled at the obvious. Keith strolled past the counter way irritated on his way to restock a box of shoes.

"Everything ok over here?" He sized Rico Suave up and down.

"Yeah, everything is fine." I nodded.

"Don't let that line get long." Keith frowned.

Meanwhile, there wasn't a line. But, I knew exactly what Keith meant. The sales team could be a little protective. That was one of the downfalls of being the only girl working in an all-men store. The guys were like older brothers to me and ran serious interference whenever any customer tried to get fresh or throw major game my way.

"I hope you enjoy your shoes." I flashed 32 pearly whites. "They're pretty dope."

"Thanks." He grinned. "You wanna go out sometime?"

"Where?" I raised a brow.

"Red Lobsters or something," He smiled. "You know, somewhere nice so I can show you a few things."

"Mmm-hmm..." I laughed. "Like what?"

"You'll see." He smirked. "Hey, take down my number."

I swiftly gave him a once over. He stood there looking cleaner than the Board of Health. *Should I entertain this guy? Is he legit?* I wondered. *Or, is he a doughboy like most of the guys who stroll through our door?* But, then I quickly remembered that he only purchased one pair of shoes. He wasn't excessive like the drug dealers who buy nothing less than five.

"So?" He interrupted my thoughts.

"Here," I immediately extracted a blank piece of paper from the register.

I quickly slid the receipt across the counter. The last thing I wanted was another run-in with Keith. I watched as he scribbled a few numbers with a signature encapsulating Winston at the bottom.

"So, it's Winston huh?" I smiled.

"Yeah," He grinned sliding the paper back over the counter. "Make sure you call."

I quickly grabbed the receipt and struggled to stuff it in the back of my fitted khakis. Winston grinned as he collected his shoes off the counter and turned to leave the store. I had to admit his lanky walk and fierce swag had me feeling some kinda way. I figured even if he was a doughboy, it wasn't like I hadn't kicked it with others before. So I'd give him a pass.

The minute I got off of work I immediately called Winston. Our phone conversation was just as electric as our first encounter. His sugary words sopped me up within a concoction of sweet bliss. We talked endlessly for most days. I was completely into Winston. Although I can't say the same for my mother, she hated him. For starters, he was a year older than me, had a car, and an aloof attitude towards parents. He also smoked marijuana like a freight train and believed in cajoling me into numerous unthinkable antics on more than one occasion. Yes, Winston was a parent's nightmare. And, like most girls, we loved the one guy our mother and father abhorred. I was no different. Winston was no good for me. God knew it. My mother knew it. Deep down inside, I knew it too. I just didn't care. I really believe free will is the most damaging gift of all at times. The brain has a way of processing information to benefit a course of action and streamline a situation to your liking. It will Rubix cube that thing to perfectly justify your decision. And, just like when a Rubix cube is stuck in a color jam, people tend to figure out a way to remove the stickers. Mechanically and strategically they're aligned in a row to fit a contrived pattern. That is exactly how the human mind operates. We manipulate, scheme, and overall want things done our way and will figure out a way to make it right even when it's wrong. Winston was my Rubix cube. I knew from day one this guy was trouble. He wreaked it. And although I reveled in hanging out at clubs and engaging in promiscuity, my friends and I somehow managed not to do drugs and we didn't drink alcohol. We drifted through those hazards effortlessly. But, I found myself falling peril to Winston. I became more deliberately disrespectful while dating him. I skipped school, stayed out all times of the night, and craved his touch like a crack-fiend craves the pipe. He explored my body in dimensions I didn't know existed and caressed me with his tongue in ways I thought unimaginable. I wanted to be with Winston every second of the day and I didn't care what mountaintop or valley below I had to tread.

True to form, Winston had a very sketchy past with not much of a future. He was a dope dealer, car thief, chop-shop laborer, and not the type of guy any girl of my caliber should have entertained. I was a Cass Technician for crying out loud. An Honor Roll student accepted into three Universities that upcoming fall. So, why was I so stupid to fall for a two-bit hustler like Winston? The answer was simple. I had an insatiable, appetite for lust. The Bible even warns in 1 Corinthians 6:18-20 (NIV), "Flee from sexual immorality. All other sins a man commits are outside his body, but he who sins sexually sins against his own body. Do you not know that your body is a temple of the Holy Spirit, who is in you, whom you have received from God? You are not your own; you were bought at a price. Therefore, honor God with your body." But I was too busy honoring my body with lust. I learned early on when the enemy discovers your vice, he will use it against you to seduce you, deceive you, and defeat you. Winston was this vice.

Senior Prom was right around the corner, High School graduation approached on the horizon, and Winston beamed as the brightest distraction on the precipice. My mother tried to warn me about wasting so much time with a guy going nowhere fast. But, I didn't listen. I didn't care. After all, I wasn't stupid. Winston was just a guy I enjoyed having fun with. I will admit I did love him. But, I didn't intend to marry him. Besides, Winston loved the streets way more than me. It was evident from his late night-runs, inconsistent calls, and lack of timeliness when we were supposed to meet. My wish was that one day Winston would awaken from his marijuana filled fog to truly realize my worth. But, I knew it wasn't likely to happen. I believed Winston cared for me. Just not enough to curb his unscrupulous behavior and street inclined ways. So, I was cool with just enjoying our numerous sexual escapades. After all, I wasn't a loose girl. And, I didn't sleep with multiple guys. This made Winston my temporary fix. Which was perfectly fine because I had bigger plans on the horizon. Once I graduated from Cass, I planned to attend Clark Atlanta

University in the fall. So, my future was bright and my radar was set to win! What could go wrong?

Summer after graduation, I found myself becoming extremely promiscuous with Winston. Oftentimes, he would hit me on my pager in the wee hours of the night. I would answer his late-night booty calls just to be swayed to leave my house. He'd convince me to jump into his car, sneak into his parent's house, and unravel in a nightcap of endless lovemaking in the sack. It was daring, adventurous, sexy, and an ultimate adrenaline rush. We loved the urgency of committing a naughty act and darting the bulls-eye of getting caught. We would laugh after our antics at how our parents were the biggest idiots in life. Winston and I thought we had it all figured out. But the only thing we figured out was how to become more sexually immersed in one another on a one-way track to disaster.

One night, I had the most disturbing dream. As usual, I was asleep in my bed. Suddenly, in the middle of the dream, my pager buzzed. I didn't answer it because my mother appeared out of nowhere and sat stoically at the foot of the bed. My pink pager buzzed again. Miraculously, within the dream state, I already knew what time it was. Readily, I sprang from the bed and dashed in a haste to get dressed. I knew it was time to meet Winston to "do what we did best". As I ran to grab the stair rail and begin my immediate descent towards the landing, my mother quickly reached out to grab my hand. Without even knowing who the caller was, what my intent could be, or where I was going; she stared dead in my eyes and whispered, "If you ever have sex in my house, I'll know." I looked at her in the dream and smiled. It was a shady smile, a slight smirk of mockery. But, my mom's demeanor remained calm, graceful, and she vocalized a second time, "I'm telling you. If you have sex in my house, you'll get pregnant." I awoke in a cold sweat. That was the weirdest dream I ever had. But, it was also a dream I never feared manifesting. For starters, why would I want to have sex in my mother's house? Gross! Plus, even if I wasn't keen on the act and location, talk about the persecution of immediate death if I was ever caught. It wasn't worth it. No sir! I'd prefer to sneak out as I've always done. After all, dirt done away from home was the cleanest dirt of all. While my dream was pretty intimidating and surreal, I knew there was nothing to fear. For starters, I didn't have time for a pregnancy. Secondly, I didn't even like kids. Plus, I only had two and a half months before I left for college and would be the hell out of Detroit. Pregnancy was definitely not on my list of things to do. Besides, Winston and I were super safe. We never had one moment of indiscretion that placed us in a risky realm. The last thing I had to worry about was a bun in the oven.

A NEW LIFE IN THE WINGS

Weeks turned into days, which turned into moments before my senior year would come to a close. Prom and graduation were a huge success! In spite of Winston and I having a huge blow up a few weeks before, which caused his imminent absence at my prom. Once he disclosed his intent to wear a ridiculous outfit, coupled with carrying a cane and cigar, I knew deep inside he would somehow screw the whole event up. Plus, he raved about how fun it would be to get high afterward. I refused to stand for that kind of embarrassment. Or, any instance of unpredictability his actions were guaranteed to bring. So, I opted to go with a platonic friend instead. Needless to say, that caused temporary pandemonium in our relationship. But, I didn't care. I knew pretty soon I would be in a different state and our relationship would hit temporary status anyway. My mother sensed the separation coming and waited anxiously in the wings.

My girlfriends Yo, Kye, Shonna, TiRiley, and I chatted nonstop about college life, pledging sororities, and newfound freedom that waited on the horizon. These girls were my squad and I loved them immensely. It was going to be hard going to a new city without my besties in tow. Yo and Kye were my day ones since middle school at Ludington while Shonna and TiRiley rolled on the scene freshman year at Cass Tech. It seemed the majority of my days were spent with my crew. We eagerly sopped up the last remnants of summer with shopping sprees, sleepovers, and crazy club excursions. Surprisingly, Winston didn't mind. He was too preoccupied making runs to the chop shop, smoking weed with his friends, and squeezing in enough time to leave a smile on my face at the end of the night with our sexual escapades. I didn't focus too much attention on Winston. Like my friends, my thoughts were consumed with college and new opportunities. There was a new life in the wings waiting for me the moment I escaped the D. I knew Winston would soon be a snapshot of my past.

Summer flew by full speed. My sister was excited about my decision to attend Clark Atlanta University in the fall since she would be a senior there as well. My grandfather beamed with joy. My mother was blissful that her two girls defeated the odds and would finally make a meaningful life away from the D. My whole family was elated. My church family even blessed me with a scholarship given my outstanding grades and award-winning essay. It seemed those years of being forced to go to church weren't in vain after all.

The countdown was on and I couldn't wait. It had been a few days since I last spoke with Winston. Honestly, I was so busy I almost didn't notice. But, one muggy Saturday night, he called.

"What up doe?" I answered

"What up doe?! Where you been?" He grilled.

"Around...Why?" I smiled.

"I want to see you."

"Aw, you miss me?" I teased.

"You can't tell?" He chuckled.

"Maybe a little." I blushed.

"Look, I know you're leaving soon and I want to kick it with you before you dip."

It had been a few weeks since we last spent time together. My schedule was slammed due to tons of graduation parties, outings with friends, and endless activities that filled my social calendar. I barely had time for him.

"That sounds fun." I cooed. "Where did you want to go?"

"Somewhere Downtown. Maybe chill at Belle Isle." He paused. "You down?"

"Bet, let's roll." I smiled.

Winston pulled up in his dark blue Chevy Caprice, sporting shiny 24-inch rims with his speakers bumping. We made headway on the Lodge expressway zooming towards downtown Detroit. I was happy he hit me up to chill, unwind, and enjoy the last few moments before I left for college. The warm summer breeze whipped through my hair as "Pretty Brown Eyes", a Mint Condition melody, bumped through the speakers. I gazed at the enormous Joe Louis' fist pumping proudly mid-air as we submerged onto Jefferson Avenue. The silver Ren Cen building towered as the Detroit River glistened in the background. We whizzed by seamless blocks of Coney Island Deli's positioned on several street corners, a signature staple for the lay of the land. I breathed in all of the city smells and sights, knowing within a few weeks, it would be a snapshot in my mind. We ascended the long narrowing bridge that crossed Jefferson Avenue leading over to Belle Isle. I peered at the Detroit skyline and gazed across the Detroit River to take in the Canadian view on the other side.

Winston and I chilled at Belle Isle for hours. We even snuggled under the stars talking endlessly about life, the future, and what would become of us once I left for college. We knew it would be difficult to advance forward as a couple. But, instead of focusing on the obvious, we simply enjoyed our time without complicating the matter with irrelevant banter. I shifted my seat and leaned further back in the car. Winston gazed directly into my eyes.

"So should we toast?"

"To what?" I asked.

"I don't know. Us...you...college." He laughed.

"With what?" I raised a brow.

"This..." He boyishly grinned and extracted a bottle of Hennessy out of a brown paper bag.

Although I was an avid non-drinker, the weeks following graduation invited all types of liquid concoctions into my slender frame. But, interestingly enough, I never drank with Winston. Therefore, I figured it only polite to enjoy a memorable libation with my sexy boyfriend as our last hoorah in Detroit. Winston opened the bottle and filled two white Styrofoam cups. Without even making an official toast, we hastily clicked cups, suggestively smiled, and took the drinks straight to the head. I felt strange. The drink was warm and strong. We took another swig. Before long, I felt outright plastered. Winston grabbed me close. Our readiness meter rose alongside our alcohol levels. We began passionately kissing nonstop in the car. Belle Isle was known as being a lover's cove where teenagers safely congregated to romp around the back seat of their car without fear of being caught. Unless of course, a Detroit Police officer patrolled the area and felt it pertinent to give an unwelcoming knock on the window. Since Winston and I found it too risky to get frisky on Belle Isle, we decided to take the party back to Bell's Lair.

We sped down the Lodge expressway and turned a couple of corners before successfully hitting Prest Street. Winston pulled a few houses down from mine, hit his lights, and turned off the ignition. We both sat outside my house seriously faded. I was fearful of him driving home in his condition. It would be safer if he just stayed with me for the night. But, the likelihood of the welcome wagon rolling in with my mother extending grace of an overnight stay was highly unlikely. I already knew she wasn't having this mess tonight. My mind hazily raced to figure out a plan that would safely incorporate Winston into the equation. Within moments, I finally concocted one.

"Listen, stay in the car." I whispered.

"Huh?" Winston slurred.

"I'm going to sneak into the house to make sure the coast is clear."

"And, then what?" He raised a brow.

"Then, all you have to do is creep up the stairs to my bedroom and crash with me until morning."

True enough, it was a crazy and daring move. But, I didn't

want to risk losing him to a DUI. Or worse yet, a fatal car crash. As far as I was concerned, this idea beat the alternative.

"How am I going to do that?" Winston looked confused.

"Easy. I'll leave the door unlocked. Just watch my bedroom window for the signal."

Skillfully, I crept in the house. It stood submerged in total blackness like a pharaoh's tomb. I quietly ascended the stairs to my room. I tiptoed towards the window and flickered my bedroom light on and off four times. Seconds later, I eagerly watched a lanky figure emerge from the car. Winston raced towards the front door. I hoped he didn't do anything dumb like trip over a random article or wake the whole household. Luckily, mission "Drink and Creep" was a huge success! Winston cautiously pushed the door handle and made his way into the Bell's lair. Fortunately, my bedroom was directly next to the front foyer so all he had to do was quietly creep up the stairs. I had to admit, it was weird having Winston in my home. He was so sexy in the moonlight filtering through the sheer bedroom curtain. He slowly climbed in bed next to me.

"Remember, no sex." I kissed him on his cheek.

"I know," he slurred assuring.

We lay cramped in my small twin bed. I nuzzled against his warm chest trying to force myself to sleep. Clearly, he was having a difficult time as well. I could feel his rock hard lower half penetrating against my thigh. It was bad enough he was in my house and in my bed. My mother would kill us if she caught us having sex. I knew I could be a pretty rebellious chick at times. But, I was determined not to break this one pivotal rule. We lay like two escaped inmates. Eyes wide agape and holding onto one another for dear life. Our adrenaline was on 20 and we were totally chartering untraveled terrains. After a moment, Winston decided he'd go in for the kill and slowly begin caressing my back. It was a soothing and innocent relief. I didn't think much of it. Until, he planted a deep passionate kiss on my lips. This was the fuel that sparked the fire. I was torn. After all, I only had a few more weeks in the D. After that, who knew when I would see him again? These were tough decisions to face at 2 a.m. with an inescapable buzz. Winston brought clairvoyance to a very confusing situation the best way he knew how. I felt him disappear and slowly descend under the sheets. He knew how to persuade me every time. Winston was going in for the win. As I enjoyed the tantalizing effect, a moment of clarity suddenly erupted. It was something about the luminance of the moonlight cascading across my bed in a dream-like haze that eerily cast a spell. I suddenly remembered my dream. *Is this how I got pregnant?* It couldn't be. Intelligence paved the way to circumvent any tragedy.

"Please tell me you have a condom." I cooed.

"Every time..." He smiled.

Protection as always, check! That's one thing I gave us credit for we were always super safe. Winston skillfully maneuvered the plastic prophylactic over his better half. We embraced like our lives depended on it. Our bodies swayed in unison in the moonlight. Winston felt amazing. I was convinced this was our best steamy moment yet. Winston held me tightly. Then, he shifted uncomfortably.

"Don't move." He cautioned.

"Why?" I hesitated.

"Hold on..."

He awkwardly stopped again.

"What's wrong?" I panicked.

"Babe..." he nervously paused.

"What?" My heart skipped a beat.

51

"The condom came off."

My heart dropped. Visions of the worst fear danced in my head. Winston used his fingers to fish deeper inside, digging and prying until he finally pulled out a ragged and torn condom. I was terrified. This couldn't happen. I refused to be pregnant. I couldn't be pregnant.

A RUDE AWAKENING

I was pregnant. Two weeks after I had totally written off that steamy night of bliss in my bedroom with Winston. I sat in a small storage space in the backroom of Foot Action USA nauseous beyond belief. My mind was as cluttered as the shoeboxes scattered all around me. I didn't understand it. It didn't make sense. Sure, lately whenever anyone hugged me my breasts throbbed in tremendous pain. But, I simply shrugged that off as they were finally beginning to grow. After all, I didn't get my period until I was 15-years-old. So, maybe that was a by-product of being a late bloomer. And yes, I stayed hungry as a hostage. But then again, I figured that could've been due to my late development as well. I mean, logically speaking, I did have an extremely high metabolism. But as my thoughts raced and this ill-feeling lingered, the nausea was a new one. I was fresh out of answers, ideas, and excuses. There was no theory I could conjure beyond the obvious. My manager Keith bolted to the back to grab a pair of shoes totally interrupting my thoughts.

"You ok?" He questioned as he witnessed me wiping tears from salt-stained cheeks.

"No, I feel sick." I sighed.

"You don't look good." He shook his head genuinely concerned. "Why don't you punch out and go home."

"Thanks Keith," I said as I tried to piece myself together.

I walked out of the mall and trudged to catch the Greenfield bus a few feet away. I braced myself for the long uncomfortable ride ahead. I couldn't go home. I needed answers now! I remembered a clinic on GrandRiver Avenue that I went to with Yo as support services a few months prior. She had to get a pregnancy test and they gave it to her for free. Her test came back negative. With any luck, I crossed my fingers and hoped my results would be the same. As my stop approached, I reached for the cord and signaled the bus driver. I nervously stood to embrace the unknown, hopped off the DOT, and filed into the small dismal clinic. I prayed that I wouldn't bump into anyone that I knew. Fortunately, it wasn't crowded. After signing in, I grabbed a seat in an old wooden chair and leaned my head against the cold wall.

"Bell..." a dark, stout, older nurse motioned for me to follow.

I apprehensively obliged. I followed her down a short hallway and halted in front of a tiny room. She ushered me inside and grabbed a clipboard with papers attached. Millions of thoughts clouded my head.

"When was your last period?" The nurse interrupted my thoughts.

"I don't remember." I sighed. "But, I know it should've come by now."

"Did you have unprotected sex?"

"Well, my boyfriend's condom came off."

"Here, take this." She handed me a small plastic cup. "The restroom is across the hall. Write your name on the cup with the marker in the stall and place it on the counter when you're done."

I grabbed the cup and headed towards the restroom a few feet away. I closed the door behind me. My mind raced. *Maybe I'm just sick. Maybe I'm not pregnant.* I exited the door slightly more confident. I placed the specimen on the counter as directed. I grabbed a seat nearby and waited anxiously. After what seemed like an eternity, the nurse reappeared. I desperately searched her face for clues. It was blank, nothing.

"Your test came back positive." She stared at me emotionlessly.

My heart sank. I went numb. The nurse's mouth moved. But, I literally didn't hear a single word. I just nodded, stood, grabbed my purse, and left.

I reluctantly boarded the bus. I filed towards the center aisle and sat motionless in my seat. A tear rolled down my cheek as I stared out the window. The reality of the situation hit harder than Mike Tyson's fist against Evander Holyfield's frontal lobe. At that moment, I would have rather volunteered for elective brain surgery with zero anesthesia than have to tell my mother I was pregnant. That news would be the bullet in a loaded gun pointed directly at her temple. Besides my mother's mental murder, if this news were to spread across the DNA pool, that would be the ultimate embarrassment to my family. Next to my sister, I was going to be the second person in my immediate family to attend college. My sister was so proud that I was going to join her down at Clark Atlanta University. That's all we talked about. A whirlwind of thoughts consumed me. How did I muscle myself into this uncanny situation? It made absolutely no sense! I can't even say I didn't see it coming. After all, the Holy Spirit even tried to warn me months in advance and I didn't listen. The Bible says in John 16:13 (NIV), "...when he, the Spirit of truth, comes, he will guide you into all truth. He will not speak on his own; he will speak only what he hears, and he will tell you what is yet to come." The more I reflected, the more it baffled my mind how the pregnancy occurred exactly how my dream and premonition predicted. I cried my eyes out coping with this newfound reality. What was I going to do? This was one of the sickest jokes God ever played on me. There were exactly seven weeks left before I was supposed to depart for college. Timing could not have been worst for a pregnancy. I had to figure out a remedy and fast! I refused to get stuck in a dead-end situation as a single mother in Detroit. Plus, I was pregnant by a drug dealing, chop-shop, hustling baby daddy. Where was the future in that? I felt like a fool! How did I not see this coming? My mother would kill me if she found out her sweet baby girl was pregnant. Surely, my grandfather would have had a heart attack on the spot. So, in order to save my family from injury, strife, and grief I did the next best thing. I held on to what attorneys refer to as the diplomatic non-disclosure. I didn't tell my mother or grandfather a single word. I couldn't bear the shame. But, time was breathing its hot breath down my neck. If I didn't do something soon, someone would uncloak my secret. I was hit with a rude awakening and had to do something fast! Given my hasty situation, an abortion seemed to be the only answer. It was a quick thing, a discreet thing, and the right thing to do. I tried to convince myself that it wasn't even a baby yet. *Right?* I needed to wipe my hands clean of this terrible mistake and start over never looking back. Nobody would even have to know.

But to my dismay, I learned that someone would definitely have to know! A representative from the abortion clinic said someone would have to drive me home. Needless to say, I didn't know who to ask. My plans were unraveling fast. I thought it was a fairly quick process. Little did I know, it wasn't swift at all. While abortions are portrayed as effortless, it is actually a serious surgical procedure. Come to find out, this quick fix wasn't as easy as I thought. My back was against the wall. I wasn't sure what to do. Against better judgment and out of desperation, I mustered enough energy to do the next best thing. I confided in my sister. I already knew her friend, Sabrina, just had one. I overheard enough of their conversations and knew I could confide in my sister about this twisted situation. I was racing against the clock and needed a remedy fast! So, my sister called Sabrina who referred me to an abortion clinic on the east side of Detroit. The cost of the procedure wasn't terribly expensive. I would have to craftily come up with the money. And, I needed an even better plan to come up with a ride considering none of us owned a car.

I n haste, I called Winston. Truth be told, he should have expected this call. After all, I complained profusely about being sick. And, I cringed in pain whenever he attempted to touch my sore breasts. Now, it was just time to confirm what we both already suspected after weeks of wishing otherwise. But, I was still extremely nervous as his home phone rang a second time. *What should I say?* A third ring. *What if he wanted to keep the baby?* A fourth ring. *What's taking him so long to answer?* Finally, the ringing ceased. I took a deep breath and anxiously paused as a voice filled the other end. I expected to hear Winston. But to my dismay, his mother answered instead.

"Hello." She cheerfully chimed.

"Hi…" I hesitated. "Mrs. Reed?"

"Who is this?" She interrupted.

"It's Tee," I paused.

"Oh Honey, Winston isn't home."

"Dang," I sighed.

"Excuse me?" She huffed.

I stood seething. Winston was supposed to answer the phone, not her. I planned this whole call in my head. Now, I felt foiled. But, desperate times called for desperate measures. I switched gears. *Midas well shoot straight from the hip.*

"Um, I don't know if Winston told you…" I paused.

"Told me what?" She cautiously replied.

"That I'm pregnant." I blurted.

"What?!"

"Pregnant," I said a second time as if she didn't hear it the first.

"Listen young lady!" She bellowed. "You and Winston are too young to be starting a family!"

"I know." I exhaled. "That's why I'm calling to get money for an abortion."

"An abortion?!" She shrieked.

"Yes," I calmly responded.

"Well, I have news for you." She breathed. "Before you do anything, I'm going to need to sit down and talk to you, Winston, and your mother!"

What??! I panicked. This plan immediately went to hell in a handbasket. The strings were unraveling fast!

"Well, my mother isn't home right now." I quickly rambled.

"When will she be?" Mrs. Reed coolly responded.

"Um, I don't know." I nervously hesitated. "I'll call you back."

"Make sure that you do."

Curses! I abruptly hung up the phone. My plan totally backfired. I couldn't believe Mrs. Reed wanted to have a pow-wow as a family. Under normal circumstances, that petition might've been ideal. However, the primary problem with her proposal stemmed from the fact that I never intended to tell my mother. Ever! Now, I was screwed. What was I going to do? I needed another course of action fast! *Who else could I call?* My mind frantically raced. Luckily, I had another card up my sleeve. With tensions mounting and desperation settling in, Lloyd quickly raced across my mind. He was an ex-boyfriend, six years my senior, dependable, and financially stable. I met Lloyd at a club the previous summer during my junior year of high school when Yo, Kye, and I snuck in. Lloyd was taking pictures as a photographer to make ends meet. He asked us to take a picture. We agreed. And, instead of charging us, Lloyd just handed it to me for free. I thought he was a really sweet guy. He and I went on a few dates here and there. We even attached the boyfriend/girlfriend title to our repertoire for a short period of time. However, things never really progressed beyond that point considering I was jailbait. Lloyd was intelligent enough to know he would find himself in serious trouble if our interactions went beyond first base. This was primarily due to the fact, I was a ripe 16 years of age and he was a very legal 22. Although, I told my mom he was 19 to take away the sting. She would've flipped her wig for sure if she knew his real age. Luckily, he looked youthful. So, it worked. The thing I appreciated best about Lloyd is he was a really cool guy and didn't seem to mind the lack of sexual intimacy. Matter of fact, he never pressured me for anything. My naive ways and innocent teen demeanor proved a turn on and he was simply satisfied enjoying my presence. Lloyd loved giving me money to buy the latest outfit, get my hair fixed, and nails did. Like most guys in the D, Lloyd fell peril to the street life. Beyond racking in the dough as a make-shift photographer, he also raked in dividends as a diligent drug dealer. I always felt he was smart, sweet, and deserved more. There wasn't anyone else in his corner cheering him towards anything positive, only me. Within time, I convinced him to go back to school and turn his life around. Lloyd was grateful for that extra push, especially considering he witnessed a few friends get murdered shortly thereafter. In the streets, loyalty begets loyalty. And Lloyd always had my back for being supportive of him in his time of need. That's why he immediately popped into the frontal lobe during my code red crisis.

Lloyd would do anything I asked at the drop of a hat within reason. But, I knew this realm of reason would prove a bit challenging. After all, he did have feelings for me and he wasn't about to support another man's mistake. He wasn't stupid. I needed to conjure a damsel in distress story and fast! That's the only way it would work. *I could easily say that I needed a physical exam before college and I didn't have health insurance. Maybe then he would let me borrow $250.* I thought. After all, $250 was chump change to Lloyd and I needed it badly. I didn't have a choice. It was the only thing that would put me one step closer to ending this horrific nightmare. The only thing I had to do now was ask.

NO QUICK FIX

It was raining outside. I piled into Lloyd's black Ford Explorer. I hadn't seen him in quite a few months. But, he looked the same with his dark midnight complexion, short stature, stocky build, and cute baby face. It became apparent almost immediately from the minute I opened the passenger door that I didn't think this plan fully through. Lloyd was elated to see me. I wish I could've said the same.

"Look at you!" He smiled reaching to give me a hug.

"Thanks for the ride." I let go of his neck. "You have no idea how much I appreciate it."

"It's all good." He leaned back in his seat. "Wait, let me give you this before I forget."

He reached in his pocket and extracted a wad of cash.

"Thanks Lloyd! I promise I'll pay you back."

"Don't worry." He grinned. You know I got you."

"I know." I shook my head thankfully.

"So what you been up to?"

"Getting ready for college. That's about it."

As simple as that sounded, I wish it would've been

completely true. But, that was the furthest thing from my reality. The truth of the matter remained that my mind was racing. It was terribly convoluted with the procedure that lay ahead.

Lloyd sped down the expressway towards the east side of Detroit. As we dashed past cars in the pouring rain it became undeniably obvious this was an awful time for a reunion. I was not prepared for Lloyd's full spread interrogation. I don't know why I assumed this ride would go smoothly. Or, even silently with minimum conversation. For some unknown reason, I foolishly thought it would be a total breeze.

"Do you know how long it's going to take?" Lloyd interrupted my thoughts.

"What?" I turned to face him.

"Your appointment."

"Not exactly." I hesitated. "But, it shouldn't be too long."

"Cool." He nodded. "What do they have to do?"

"I'm not sure," I mumbled. I felt a little better knowing at least that part was true.

"Well, hopefully you'll get your results today or in time for school."

I had to admit. I was becoming increasingly annoyed. I was already exhausted and we hadn't even made it to the clinic. Luckily, our exit was fast approaching and Lloyd would have to focus more on the road and a lot less on my issues. As we turned a few corners, a very small, obscure, and badly faded white building appeared in the distance. I remembered Sabrina saying I'd see a white building the minute we got off of the expressway.

"That's it right there." I pointed as Lloyd swerved to the side.

"You sure," he raised a brow.

"I think so." I became equally disturbed as we advanced closer.

The structure was so dilapidated I was stunned the health department didn't warrant it a hazard and have it burned to the ground. *Surely this couldn't be the clinic.* I looked down at the address scribbled on my small notepad and noticed the numbers were identical.

"Yep, that's it." I nodded.

I didn't want to step foot inside this place. But, desperate times called for desperate measures. I was already present and didn't have time to be picky.

We filed inside the clinic. My nerves stood on end. This was the oddest phenomenon in life. I couldn't believe that I was sitting in a clinic with my ex-boyfriend. One with whom I've never had sex. Meanwhile, he was funding my abortion under the pretense it was a physical exam. Needless to say, this situation was a hot mess! For starters, it was completely shady. Secondly, it would be a disaster if Lloyd ever found out the truth. I could not wait for this nightmare to end.

"Bell..." A portly nurse with soft golden hair called my name.

I stood nervously and shuffled towards her. The nurse quickly whisked me down a long hallway and placed me in a room where 10 girls sat crowded in a small bleak space. It was a terrifying scene. The majority of the girls were white with the exception of two black girls. No one appeared to be over the age of 18-years-old. Matter of fact, many looked to be around 16-years-old with the youngest girl right around the tender age of 12 wearing a mouthful of braces. Mutually, we shared the expression of fear, anxiety, and shame. I remembered thinking surely the conditions should not be like this. It seemed as if we were young pregnant heifers being herded to slaughter. The atmosphere was cold, uncertain, and unwelcoming.

"Fill this out," a slender white nurse with dark black hair and a mean streak said in an agitated tone. She handed me a clipboard. "You'll need to take these too." She issued two pills.

I was confused. I needed an adult. Suddenly, this did not seem like a good idea. But, then I remembered the alternative. Stay pregnant, stay home, forfeit college, and live a doomed life. I filled out the form, handed it to the nurse, and was instructed to hand over $250 cash at once. I thought that was a bit odd. Shouldn't you pay after the procedure? Shouldn't I be able to communicate with a doctor first? The whole process was surreal. I hated this place. Why would Sabrina refer me to this dump? I wanted to go home! But, the nurse instructed that I follow her down another narrow hallway instead. I was petrified and beginning to question my decision every step of the way. *On second thought, maybe having a baby wasn't so bad.* This place was giving me the creeps. The nurses were heartless. And, I could not escape the thought of why did they have so many young girls crammed in a room popping pills? *Was this place even legal?!* Before I could let my thoughts get the best of me, the same skinny nurse with jet black hair and even darker eyes led me into a large white room. She motioned towards a stretcher and told me to get undressed. I had the most difficult time pulling out of my clothes. My legs felt like sandbags. As I approached the stretcher, I noticed several droplets of blood on the floor next to the table. Surely, that couldn't be sanitary. I immediately felt nauseous and seriously grossed out beyond belief. With every step, I completely questioned my decision and whether to make a last-minute retreat. And if the blood wasn't bad enough, worst still, a girl in the next room began moaning piercingly. This freaked me out even more. I sat on that cold bed in a flimsy gown completely shaken. My thoughts raced. Suddenly, there was commotion in the next room.

"NOOOOOOOOO!!!!" The girl shrieked. "Stop! It hurts!"

What the... I looked around the room terrified. A small voice inside of me calmly said, *"Leave now."* Like lightning, I jumped off the table and darted to grab my clothes lying on the chair. Instantaneously, the nurse with the dark eyes bolted into the room, startled to see me reaching for my pants.

"What are you doing?" She walked towards me.

"I don't think I want to do this anymore," I quivered.

"It's ok. You just need to get back on the table." She coaxed. "Everything will be all right."

"Then why is that girl screaming?!" I demanded.

"The girl next door is a problem child. She's been here several times before." The nurse placed her hands on my shoulder. "It doesn't hurt. Believe me. The doctor is a professional. You're in good hands."

I didn't want to believe her. I was horrified out of my mind.

"I think I want to leave," I pleaded.

But as I supplicated, an older Indian male, Dr. Sanjay, with medium height, and a reserved demeanor entered the room. "It's okay you need to get back up on the table." He nodded.

I didn't know what to do. Reluctantly, I climbed back on

the slab, lay on my back, and stared at the ceiling. I didn't feel good about any of this.

Dr. Sanjay utilized an ultrasound machine and prodded about. I wondered what he was looking at. I didn't see anything but shades of white, black, and gray on the monitor. I was certain I'd see a baby or something. I wasn't even sure what to look for. Would it even be a full baby or just perhaps a dot? He prodded for a while. *Should it take this long?* I nervously thought.

"Is everything ok?" I inquired.

"Yes." He soothed. "How many weeks are you?"

"Six weeks," I lied.

"Oh, ok." He raised a brow and continued prodding away with the device.

Truthfully, I was only five weeks. But, I figured what difference could seven days make? School started in two weeks and I was pressed for time.

"Do you see a baby?" I asked.

Dr. Sanjay totally disregarded my question. He seemed to get irritated with my inquiry as if I were questioning his professionalism. He didn't even respond to my concern, let alone offer any information as to what he was doing. His attitude was arrogant and unabashed. I stared at the dark monitor confused. I couldn't make out any of it. I tried to relax as best as I could. My anxiety was getting the best of me.

"Let's get started." Dr. Sanjay placed the ultrasound to the side and motioned to the nurse.

She handed him a long menacing device. I was instructed to keep my legs ajar as the mechanism was turned on and the loud hum from the machine vibrated the floor. This ordeal was immensely painful. Dr. Sanjay jabbed unmercifully inside of my uterus sucking the life from under of me. I wanted to go home. The torment was treacherous, dreadful, and it felt as if my soul was being vacuumed from between my legs. I wanted to die. Emptiness, filth, and an unsettling gut intuition permeated the chambers of my brain. This whole experience didn't feel right. I wanted out.

"All done," Dr. Sanjay proudly proclaimed once the machine calmed.

I felt rotten and deeply disturbed. The nurse ushered me to another room. I was told I would need to be monitored before finally being discharged from this hellish ordeal. I sat there perplexed. Instead of feeling whole, I felt broken. There was definitely no quick fix to this situation. The decision I thought to be best turned into a nightmare. I didn't feel relieved, nor good, or sound. I just wanted to go to sleep and wake up from this dreadful dream. The only problem was it was no dream, only my horrid reality.

I met Lloyd in the lobby. There was something about his expression that insinuated he knew more than I gave him credit for. Perhaps, it was the long wait or my disheveled and discontented demeanor. We drove home in silence. I was cramping terribly. But, I was determined to make lemonade out of lemons and put this ghastly misfortune behind me. In less than two weeks, I'd be in Atlanta. Surely, things would have to be better down there. My fingers were crossed.

SECRETS

My mother, grandmother, and I hit the open highway zooming down I-75 South headed towards Atlanta. Thick billowy clouds, gentle sun rays, and a warm breeze served as a bright pathway championing a better life ahead. My mother and grandmother both giggled like schoolgirls as they told stories, shared past experiences, and eagerly championed the 12-hour road-trip ahead. Pure exuberance shone from my mother's face as she gleefully proclaimed that her little girl had made it. Her youngest daughter was about to be a college freshman. She couldn't have been more proud. My mom's bragging rights instantaneously doubled with two girls in college. Suddenly, I felt guilty for all of the mayhem, worry, and grief I put her through as a bratty and disrespectful teen matriculating through high school just a few months prior. I stared at the woman who raised me for the past 18 years. I barely noticed how a few strands of silver caressed the corners of her otherwise youthful face. Her mouth spoke words. But, I didn't hear them. She laughed with my grandmother. But, I didn't understand the joke. Clearly, there was a conversation being had. But, in my thoughts all I heard was silence. I stared out of the window, glancing back periodically at my grandmother and mother's incessant chatter. While I was ecstatic to go to college, I was still very much torn with my inner demons. I just terminated a baby. Somehow all of my sexual escapades, reckless behavior, and disobedience began to affect my spirit. As religiously rebellious as I had become, I was still smart enough to realize my life was blessed. I graduated from Cass Tech with honors. I was accepted into Clark Atlanta University. I escaped the clutches of Detroit to create a better life for myself in Atlanta. But, spiritually, I felt lost. I wasn't that close to God to begin with. And, I was certain he hated me now after the abortion. I had no idea how to get back on a close footing with him even if I tried. I stared at the big billowy clouds. I wanted to pray but I wasn't quite sure what to say. I closed my eyes and let out a sigh. *I'm sorry* was the only thing I could muster. There was no rainbow that broke the heavens, or a cloud with a huge thumbs up, or even a dove carrying an olive branch that flew by the window to signal he heard my petition. All I heard was crickets. There is a powerful verse in the Bible. Proverbs 28:13 (KJV) says, "He that covers his sins shall not prosper; but whoso confesseth and forsaketh them shall have mercy." I could only hope that held true for my sin of abortion. I figured my lackluster apology to God would serve as a confession thereby granting leniency. But, somehow deep inside, I seriously doubted it. I mean you can't just live carefree, commit countless sins, and then at the drop of a hat confess and have them washed away. That would be a bit hypocritical, right? I was so tormented in my thoughts that I didn't know what to believe. But, I hoped I would be given a pass anyhow.

I stared out at the beautiful Midwestern horizon before us. My mother beamed with pride. It was no surprise she struggled on and off the system raising three children by herself. My little brother, Jay, was four years old and my mother had no job, which meant a brand new struggle about to begin. But, at least her girls were going to be all right. My mother was so proud of me. I was enthusiastic to be attending college. But, I wasn't proud of myself. I felt tainted. I wasn't the perfect image of the model created by my family. But, I had to still pretend and uphold this image as if I were. Luckily, after the abortion my sister didn't rat me out. She held onto her title as the black sheep of the family for the many past occurrences and situations she found herself in. Secretly, no one in my family even thought that she would attend college. I think she strived harder just to prove them all wrong. But, on the flip side of that coin, I was expected to go. I was considered the goody-two-shoes in the family and donned the honor roll kid. The truth was, I did dirt and lots of it. Fortunately enough, my dirt just never came to light. But, my sister knew the biggest mud-hole of all. If ever she wanted to lose her black sheep title, this was the perfect time to pass the torch. But she didn't. I was thankful to her for that. However, the guilt and pressure still weighed in on me. I was no longer the blemish-free, perfect, smart, and talented daughter. That was a hard pill to swallow. I drove down the highway with that secret held close to my bosom. I remembered hearing in Sunday school the Bible warned in St. Luke 8:17 (KJV), "For nothing is secret, that shall not be made manifest; neither anything hid, that shall not be known and come abroad." But, I was certain that I didn't have anything to worry about. I was sure my sister would take this secret to the grave.

As Earth Wind and Fire played in the background and sunrays dashed rapidly through tree branches, I thought of all of my friends back home I would miss. The night before, I talked for hours to Yo, Kye, Shonna, and TiRiley. Interestingly enough, I never called Winston back since the day that I hung up on his mother. I even left Detroit without telling him goodbye. Needless to say, he never contacted me either. I'm sure his family charged my call as a fake pregnancy scare with hopes of swindling them out of cash. Many girls were scandalous like that in the D. But, that wasn't my case. Sadly, neither Winston nor his parents cared enough to follow up to even see what became of my decision. They didn't even call to check to see if I was ok. Luckily, none of that mattered anymore. Like my abortion, Winston would soon be a part of my past.

FRESHMAN WEEK

College life was amazing! Clark Atlanta University's campus spiraled with several large academies, numerous dorm rooms, Greek staples on the yard, a historic landscape, and many famous landmarks shot in Spike Lee's movie "School Daze" and several other notable films. I was mesmerized and excited all the same. I met so many people from various parts of the country and truly looked forward to jump-starting my college experience. As we perused the campus grounds, my mother cheerfully informed me that she received a call from family in Cleveland, Ohio. Apparently, my cousin Nikki received an athletic scholarship to Clark and was attending as a freshman as well. That was pretty exciting news considering I hadn't seen Nikki since we were both little girls. Although we were slated to stay in separate dorms, I still looked forward to bumping into her on the yard at some point. I wondered if she looked the same or would I even recognize her? I knew one thing for sure Clark was guaranteed to be a total blast with my sister and cousin on campus.

My sister drove into Atlanta a few weeks earlier to

handle a housing crisis since Clark failed to properly apply her housing credit. Although she was irritated by the inconvenience, I was pleased all the same. It gave us an opportunity to bond before school started. Otherwise, I would have to figure out the campus on my own until she arrived a few weeks later. Kita eagerly met with the family to give a brief campus tour and escort us to my new residence otherwise known as Merner Hall. I climbed the stairwell of this large older building with pride. I was elated to discover that my sister shared the same dorm just three years earlier. But, I was surprised there wasn't an elevator or escalator to make the ascension easier. Then again, Merner was built in the '40s. So, I suppose I would have to give my new home a pass. We tackled three flights of stairs and approached a slender door with a welcome board attached. I eagerly thrust the door wide open. I had to admit my new room was much smaller than I anticipated, especially considering I would have to share the same space with someone else. But, I quickly brushed off the discontent and walked over to the wall to search for a thermostat to blast some cold air.

"There is no air conditioning." My sister laughed.

"Are you serious?!" My eyes widened in disbelief.

I stood in the middle of the room already seemingly filled to capacity with my mother, grandmother, sister, and myself. There were two twin beds cradling opposite sides of the wall with two wooden desks resting at the end of both headboards. There was little room left to the imagination given it was approximately 200 square feet at best. I scanned the area totally optimistic and already envisioning a myriad of posters and CAU paraphernalia that I planned to smear across my side of the room. I strolled over to the large windowpane facing the north side of campus in hopes of grasping a soft breeze.

"Just be prepared to take at least two to three showers a day." My sister smiled.

"For real?!"

"Yep!" She grinned. "It gets really hot. But, you'll get used to it."

"I guess." I smirked.

"Welcome to Clark!" She beamed.

At that moment, it didn't matter that the room was sweltering and I lacked air conditioning. Or, that my room was tiny and space compromised. All in all, I was just happy to be in Atlanta and excited to call the dorm home. As my family chatted and began to make one half of the room more vibrant, my roommate, Dia, strolled through the door. She was a bit on the shy side, sported a short Halle Berry haircut, and stood a spirited 4 inches shorter than me. Which wasn't saying a whole lot considering I was pretty petite and stood only a few inches over 5 feet. I hoped she was cool because I'd detest being cramped in a tiny space with someone I hated. After all, I already knew I could be a handful to deal with. This space wasn't big enough to maintain two large personalities. Luckily, my roommate was really nice. She drove down from Maryland with her grandmother and father. Our families chatted up a storm while Dia and I became acclimated. Whenever my sister joined in the conversation and wanted to get Dia's attention, she just took the liberty of calling her Lil D. And somehow from that point, the nickname like glue just stuck. True to form, Lil D and I were total opposites. She was really reserved, wanted to be a doctor, and had a laid-back personality. I, on the other hand, was incredibly outgoing, a Mass Communications major, and planned to study film. Lil D and I formed an immediate friendship. She was super cool and we were inseparable from day one.

My sister was pressed for time since she only came down to handle a housing mishap on campus. I wish she could've stayed longer. But, given we didn't have much time. Kita decided to give me and Lil D a brief tour of the city so we would know a few cool spots to hit. We drove through downtown Atlanta taking in all of the sights the city had to offer. I was mesmerized by the tall skyscrapers, the cleanliness of the city, and the true southern hospitality displayed by the residents. As we drove down the expressway, we approached a very large grayish-looking structure. It kind of reminded me of a bigger version of the Jeffries Projects that sat alongside the expressway back home in Detroit.

"What's that?!" I pointed.

"Where?" Kita turned.

"Right there," I motioned.

"Oh, that's Grady." She said.

"Is it the projects?" I winced.

"Girl, naw!" She laughed. "It's a hospital."

"Oh." I raised a brow. "Well, that's good to know."

"No, it's not!" Her expression fell flat.

"Why?" I questioned.

"Believe me, you don't ever want to go there," She paused. "People die there."

Unfortunately, it looked like it too. It was a rather large, drab, and run-down building. I definitely made sure to place it on my mental note of places to never go.

By the time we made it back to Merner Hall, my mom had finished loading up the car and she was ready for the troupe to head back to Detroit. We all hugged, kissed, and bid our farewells. I didn't know what to expect being in a new city, alone. My sister wouldn't return for another week since seniors didn't have to be on the yard until much later. It was a bittersweet departure. But, one that was necessary in order for me to grow wings and fly. I was so ready to start a new life. In Atlanta, the sky was the limit.

Lil D and I attended various Freshman Week activities, lectures, ice-breakers, and the list goes on. By Thursday, we were totally acclimated to our new surroundings. There was a huge AUC Block party on Morris Brown's Campus that day. A few of my friends from the dorm including Little D, and I went. We were on the football field in the blistering heat eating hotdogs, joking, flirting with the guys, and taking in the sights. We were truly having the time of our lives.

"Race you to the top!" I yelled to Lil D motioning towards the bleachers.

"Let's do it!" She welcomed the challenge.

"Go!" I shouted.

Running full speed and not getting very far, we both reached the metal rails, laughing, tired, and out of breath. I munched on the last morsel of my hot dog as Lil D and I plopped down on the bleachers. I scanned the field in hopes to spot our new dorm sisters Angelica and Denise. Angelica was a short spunky girl from Chicago. She always wore mid-drift tank tops and signature baggy jeans resembling Left Eye from

TLC. Denise was Angelica's polar opposite with sun-kissed skin, full-figured physique, and around the way girl persona. Although Denise was clearly the same age as the rest of us, she seemed more like an older auntie with her nurturing demeanor and ever-faithful cigarette dangling from the corner of her lip. Both girls were super chill and Lil D and I frequented the dining hall with them. So, it only seemed right for all of us to attend the close of Freshmen Week activities together. As soon as I saw Denise and Angelica appearing in the distance, I stood to signal our comrades over to the bleachers. But as I rose, I suddenly felt extremely lightheaded and promptly fell back into my seat.

"You, ok?" Lil D looked concerned.

"Yeah, I'm fine." I heaved. "Just dizzy. Must be the heat."

The weather in Georgia was no joke! It was hot as Hades and the name HotLanta was adequately given to this sweltering Metropolis. I didn't feel good. I hoped it wasn't food poisoning.

"D, I need to get back to the dorm."

"Why?" She looked bummed.

"It's too hot out here. I feel sun sick or something."

"It's cool. Let's go." She helped me up.

That was Lil D, always reliable, easy-going, and go with the flow. I admired her calm demeanor and laid back personality. We were becoming really close friends and did nearly everything together. You rarely saw one without the other. I was truly happy Lil D wasn't pissed when I was ready to leave the block party to head back to the dorm. Naturally, the other girls weren't ready to part ways with the fiesta. So, we left them at Mo Brown to enjoy the rest of the events. It seemed all the freshmen week activities from rising at the crack of dawn every day to partying until the wee hours of the morning were starting to take a toll on me. I felt completely drained. The walk back to the dorm was no fun either. I kept pausing along the way with a penetrating woozy sensation. This Georgia heat was raking me across the coals. I didn't realize we stayed at Morris Brown as long as we did. By the time we made it back to the dorm, dinner would soon be served. Lil D and the girls were ready to make tracks to the mess hall. But, instead of joining them, I passed. I lay down to take a nap and prayed that I would feel much better when I awoke. I didn't know why I felt so sick. The more I thought about it, I probably shouldn't have eaten that hot dog earlier. I sure hope it wasn't food poisoning.

FOLLOW ME

I awoke abruptly out of my sleep. I didn't realize I was knocked out for hours! My dorm room was dark, muggy, and still. I saw Lil D, peacefully resting on the other side of the room in her small twin bed. My eyes shifted uncomfortably in the darkness. A soft buzzing hissed through the plastic fan cradling the window. D shifted momentarily. She looked so serene with her head peeking from under the covers. I wish I could say the same. My body felt like it was hit by a freight train. My stomach twisted in pain, the same as it had hours earlier on the football field. Only, this time worse! My mouth became increasingly dry. I felt my entire torso succumbing to terrible agony. Sweat trickled down my forehead. My eyes hysterically darted to and fro. Only instants remained before I would hurl in the worst kind of way. *Oh no here it comes! Where's the trashcan?* I thought. I fumbled through the darkness knocking over everything in sight. Pain shot down my side. I tried to raise myself out of bed. But, the pain was too severe. I could only rummage through clothes, books, and a stack of folders in my immediate surroundings.

A textbook fell from the foot of the bed with a loud thump waking Lil D. I continued to anxiously search in the dark. I had to find it and fast!

"You, ok?!" A quizzical Lil D sat upright in her bed staring at me intently.

"No! I gotta throw up!" I wailed.

Where's the freaking trashcan?! I panicked. I searched and searched. In the nick of time, I found it stashed right behind my bed. Like a volcano about to erupt, I shot forth all the contents weighing in on my belly. But, nothing much came up except thick liquidity mucus. I sat back on the bed heaving again. More vomit erupted. Instead of feeling better, I felt worse! The sharp aches were excruciating. It felt as if King Kong towered above me and delivered blow after blow of massive non-stop uppercuts to the gut.

"Tee! Tee!!" Lil D screamed.

I stared blankly back. As much as I wanted to respond, I couldn't. I opened my parched mouth. But no words came out. I leaned against the bed. I tilted my head towards the ceiling. I blacked out.

When I came to, a sea of people surrounded my tiny dorm space. Paramedics were frantically yelling orders and rushing about. I was able to hazily identify the robust frame of the Resident Advisor from next door. I also witnessed a terrified Lil D crying hysterically on her bed. I lay still, confused, and too frail to pull down my oversized t-shirt barely covering my delicate flower exposed to all of the strangers and pandemonium surrounding me. *What was going on?!* I had no clue. The only thing I knew for sure was that my body was engulfed in severe agony and something was terribly wrong. A young white girl, wearing a paramedic jacket with piercing blue eyes and a blonde ponytail broke my train of thought.

"What's your name?!" Medic Girl keenly stared into my eyes.

"Tee…" I weakly replied.

"Where are you from?" She quickly fired.

"Detroit…" I heaved.

My throat was extremely parched and my lips were dry. The medical team worked diligently alongside her. Sharp pangs stabbed my stomach. The pain was unbearable. I wanted to go to sleep so badly. I was incredibly tired.

"When is your birthday?" Medic Girl grilled.

"January…" I whispered through the pain.

"Where are you from?"

Now, this was getting silly. She just asked me that. I was becoming irritated and my stomach was killing me!

"I'm tired." I moaned. "I just want to go to sleep."

"You can't go to sleep..." Her eyes widened. "Stay with me sweetie…"

Medic 2, a tall white male, with dark hair, and intense dark eyes rushed to her side. While Medic 3, a younger male, with a blonde crew cut assisted.

"Pulse?!" Medic 2 snapped reaching around me.

"Dropping!" Medic 3 intently held my arm shouting a series of numbers.

"My stomach hurts!" I cried. "Please just let me go to sleep!"

"You gotta stay awake…" Medic Girl warned. "One more time, sweetie, when is your birthday?"

Now, I was becoming angry! Why was she asking the

same ridiculous questions over and over? And, why couldn't she get this information from the Resident Advisor or even Lil D? I needed help! I could barely concentrate with the sharp stabs shooting through my lower abdomen. I didn't want to answer any more questions. I just wanted these people out of my room. I wanted all this yelling to stop. I wanted the pain to go away. And, I was so tired. I rolled to my side. *That's it!* I wasn't cooperating anymore. *To hell with this!* I was going to sleep.

"You can't go to sleep!" Medic Girl pleaded. "You have to stay awake!" She quickly flipped me back.

"Pulse?!" Medic 2 shouted.

"Dropping fast..." Medic 3 warned as the numbers recounted became lower.

"Tee!" She shrieked. "Stay with me!"

"Pulse?!" Medic 2 shouted.

"She doesn't have one!" Medic 3 panicked. "I...I don't have a pulse..."

The voices in the room suddenly grew lower and lower. Almost as if someone took the knob on a radio and rotated it backward so the volume turned from the loudest decimal to the lowest. It was the strangest phenomenon considering I knew there were tons of people in my room. But, I didn't understand as I began to close my eyes why their voices became fainter. Even visually, the images before me didn't just disappear as they normally would when you close your eyes. Instead, it looked as if everything in the room drifted further and further away as if I were being pulled in one direction and the entire room in another. I felt my body sinking backward and my whole surroundings suddenly grew black; pitch black. I didn't hear anyone anymore. I couldn't see anything either. But, I was totally conscious and knew something was wrong. I couldn't see my body. But, it felt as though I was still lying on my back. Everything was completely still around me. The dense air was frigid and exceedingly cold. But, surprisingly it wasn't uncomfortable. Matter of fact, it felt great! My entire body was engulfed in an incredible sense of peace, an unexplainable comfort, and I was in absolutely zero pain! My mind rapidly pondered in this obscure dark world. *How was this possible?! Where did everyone go? Why can't I hear anyone? And, why is it I don't feel any more pain?* At that instant, my body shot forward at the speed of light in this dark black abyss. *Oh no!* I panicked. *I'm dying! I'm dying!!* I sped faster and faster ahead within this passageway. The icy air caressed my cheeks and brushed against my body as I rapidly shot forward. A light whirring sound permeated past my ear canals as my body plunged deeper and faster ahead. It was similar to how the wind hums when you're speeding in a car with the windows down. Only, this whooshing sound wasn't irritating. There was no commotion of background noise only the soothing caress of air as I shot faster and faster forward. It's wild, how you have no idea what to expect when you're dying. But, one thing I never anticipated was to be totally conscious in the midst of it. Like, my mind was one hundred percent coherent. I was aware of everything around me. I just couldn't physically grab my body. Yet, I could feel my form soaring forward. The one key sensation I felt as I darted into the unknown was a sense of peace, the eradication of pain, and the soothing calmness that embraced my body. It was absolutely wonderful! But, just as I was ready to submerge and totally succumb to the sensation of utopia, I was suddenly gripped with fear. *Where was I headed?* I had no clue. I lived so waywardly that I was totally apprehensive of this moment. The reality is, in the whole scheme of things, I didn't have much good to account for. I mean sure I excelled in school. But, I don't think God cared much about grades. As my mind raced, my body jolted forward even faster. I didn't see a light ahead. There were no ancestors or friendly faces smiling to greet me. I remembered hearing people on television speak of bright lights and welcoming spirits in their near-death experiences. I didn't see any of that. I didn't hear anything. *Where was I going?!* I panicked. The only good working in my favor was the fact that I was in absolutely zero pain. But, I was still afraid. I remembered all of the times I misbehaved and lived a reckless lifestyle. All of the sex, sneaking, lying, and defiance. *Was I going to hell?!* Suddenly, my body came to an abrupt halt! Everything was motionless, still, and dark. That's when he spoke to me. I heard the voice of God! His voice was soothing, yet powerful, and omnipresent. It didn't flow from one direction, like when humans speak to one another. Instead, it thunderously resonated from all four corners: north, south, east, and west simultaneously. It rolled like commanding waters yet was gentle as a summer's breeze. His voice was celestial. It was omnipotent. It was powerful. And, it was God. God's voice was like no voice I had ever heard in my entire life. His voice was universal just like his presence. The best way I can describe it, it's like you're standing in a very large pitch-black theater with Dolby surround sound all by yourself. His voice literally came from every angle and it had depth and dimension, not just sound. See, as human beings, we only know our five senses to hear, see, touch, taste, and smell. I realized there are so many levels of complexities in the spiritual realm. The voice of God is not as simple as our sense of hearing. You cannot only hear it, but you can feel it as well. It reverberated with power. It sounded enormous and

I felt minuscule. I was mesmerized and gripped with fear all the same. I didn't know what was coming next or what to expect. But, God didn't come forward with a long lecture. And, he didn't chastise me about my indiscretions. Instead, the words he spoke were short, deliberate, to the point, and profound. He declared four words and four words only. Yet, those four words were the most powerful words that shook me to my core. Unwaveringly and directly he commanded, "***Follow me my daughter***." And, upon hearing his last word, my body shot backward full speed! I bolted faster and faster just as quickly as I had initially soaring forward. I didn't know what was happening. Or, how it was even possible. The air was still piercing cold. My surroundings were still pitch black. And, my body blasted backward at the speed of light.

CONFESSIONS

My eyes popped open.

"She's back!" Medic Girl shrieked.

"It hurts!!!" I screamed.

The pain hit my body a thousand times harder than it had before! I went from zero pain in that black abyss to unbearable agony now.

"What's your name?" Medic Girl repeated the drill.

"Tee..." I winced through the pangs.

I realized now, they didn't want me to fall asleep for fear of imminent death. I had to stay awake. I couldn't go back to sleep. This time, I cooperated to the full extent even though the pain was excruciating.

"Where are you from?" Medic Girl fired.

"Detroit..." I heaved.

"Pulse??! Medic 2 drilled.

"Low..." Medic 3 fired numbers.

"We gotta get her out of here!" Medic 2 demanded.

"Where's the stretcher?!" Medic Girl shrieked.

"In the truck..." Medic 3 shouted.

"We don't have time!" Medic 2 warned.

"We can wrap her in this!" Medic Girl motioned towards the bedsheets.

I was terribly weak and still clueless as to what was going on. Lil D was crying uncontrollably on her bed as our Resident Advisor wrapped her thick arms around Lil D and held her close. The medics grabbed my bed sheet as I lay flat within and folded it at the top. They quickly gripped their fair share, darted out of the room, and dashed down three flights of stairs. The paramedics bolted through the heavy front door and holstered me into the ambulance parked right outside.

It was the wee hours of the morning as the ambulance zoomed down the street. In the truck, I found myself connected to all kinds of monitors. The medics performed various checkpoints as they diligently charged towards their destination determined not to lose me again.

"She's complaining that her stomach hurts." I heard Medic 2 shout over the loudspeaker.

"When was your last period?" Medic Girl gently peered into my eyes.

I had no clue. Actually, I hadn't even thought about it considering it was pretty abnormal since it first began.

"June, I think." I whispered.

"Are you pregnant?" Medic Girl hesitantly inquired.

"No." I heaved.

The paramedics continued speaking to the dispatcher at the hospital. As we whizzed down the expressway, I caught a small glimpse of a large gray structure looming in the distance. It read Grady Memorial Hospital. All I could hear was my sister's voice methodically saying, "You don't ever want to go there. People die there."

The medical team rushed me in a stretcher down the hallway of Grady Hospital full steam. I fixated on the grayish-white walls, dim lights flashing overhead, and people's startled expressions as they leaped out of the pathway, dashing to the side, and literally parting the hallway like the Red Sea. We rounded a few corners and I could see the emergency OB-GYN ward clear in the distance. The medics ushered me into a room where a thin lady in a white doctor's coat approached us. She had welcoming blue eyes, flaxen blonde curls, and a concerned expression.

"This is the patient we called about." Medic Girl volunteered.

"I'm Dr. Klein, what's going on?" She raised a brow.

"We don't know. She's complaining that her stomach hurts." Medic Girl paused. "She said she's not pregnant. But, she hasn't had a period since June. So, we're dropping her off with you."

"Okay set her up over there." Dr. Klein pointed to an adjoining room.

This was the most bizarre experience I ever had in my life. I was confused beyond belief and extremely weak. Dr. Klein hooked me up to all kinds of monitors and even rolled an ultrasound in the room. She prodded and poked all around. Surprisingly, the screen looked just as it did at the abortion clinic. There was grayish-white matter all around, some black hues, but nothing else on the screen.

"I'm not pregnant..." I feebly mumbled.

"When was your last period?" Dr. Klein questioned.

"I don't know." I stared at the ceiling.

"The Medics said it was in June."

"I know. But, I'm not pregnant." I weakly added.

Dr. Klein ignored my input and continued prodding with the ultrasound.

"Hmm…" she paused. "This is interesting…I don't see anything." She stated a little above a whisper.

She moved the ultrasound to the side and jotted down a few notes.

"I'll be right back." She motioned.

Dr. Klein left the room for what felt like an eternity. I had to pee and bad!

"Doctor!" I weakly yelled.

But no one came.

"Doctor…" I called a second time in vain.

Still, no one came. I didn't want to pee on myself lying in the bed. That would have been an embarrassing state of affairs. I had no idea where the nurse was. And, there were IV tubes all over my arm. I wasn't sure how I was going to do this. But, after a quick analysis, I assumed it would be best to just try to manage and walk with the IV still attached. I slowly pushed back the thin sheets covering my abdomen. My suffering was insurmountable. I mustered an inkling of energy to raise myself up and swayed my legs off of the stretcher. Every move I made caused thunderbolts of pain to shoot down my abdomen. I grabbed the neck of the IV stand and began to slowly walk towards the adjacent door, leading to the bathroom. I gazed down at the square tiles to focus my next steps. I slowly lifted one foot in front of the other. Suddenly, everything went black.

I awoke to a shrill scream. *What happened?!* I quizzically gazed around the room. Apparently, I never made it to the bathroom. Dr. Klein rushed over and collected me off the floor.

"What were you trying to do?!" She frantically yelled.

"I was trying to go to the bathroom…" I stammered.

"Don't ever do that again! Do you hear me?!" She scolded.

"But, I had to go." I pleaded.

"You could have seriously hurt yourself. Your IV could've ripped out of your arm!"

Dr. Klein anxiously propped me back in the bed and immediately forced a catheter between my legs.

"Don't move. Got it?" She looked more worried than angry.

I nodded. She immediately began looking at the ultrasound again.

"This doesn't make sense. I don't know why I don't see anything." She shook her head clearly puzzled.

Dr. Klein prodded a bit more still speaking aloud.

"Well, I guess I'll tell them to take you to another ward. It must be something else."

Dr. Klein began unhooking the ultrasound. My mind was racing. I thought I'd never have to face my worst fear. I definitely didn't want to verbally make any kind of confessions about the mistakes that I made. But, what if this was something that she needed to know? What if I was supposed to say something?

"Doctor…" I weakly whispered.

"Yes…" she looked perplexed.

"I had an abortion a few weeks ago..." I could barely muster enough energy to get the words out.

"Oh God!" Her eyes bulged. "We have to get you to surgery now!"

What?! This was not the response I expected. Dr. Klein

hastily exited the room and returned just as quickly with a stack of papers.

"Sign this!" She shoved the forms into my hand.

I didn't understand any of it. Nothing was explained. I still had no clue what was happening. Surgery seemed so major. Shouldn't my mother be here to help with this decision?

"What if I don't want surgery?" I was exhausted from the whole ordeal and trying to exert a sense of independence at the most inopportune time.

"Listen!" She frantically placed her face so close to mine that our noses almost touched. "You either sign this paperwork or you're going to die!" she shrieked.

It didn't sound like I had much choice in the matter. So, I obliged. But, I was too weak to sign my name. I could only muster enough strength to draw a huge X on each page as she flipped through. A medical team appeared at my side in the blink of an eye and whizzed my bed down the long corridor. People leaped to the side as the medics dashed past. I stared at the dingy walls, the flickering lights, and thought once again I was not about to make it. My sister might be right after all. I could never imagine in my wildest dreams anything happening quite like this. Plus, when you line all the dots in a row, I was still clueless to all the facts leading me down this very strange rabbit hole. All I knew was my stomach felt like it was about to explode! I was incredibly weak. And apparently, I fainted more times than I can remember. Now, I was being faced with surgery or imminent death. What a crazy week. College just started and I had only been in Atlanta for a total of seven days! Plus, my family had no idea where I was or what was happening to me. It wasn't fair. I didn't understand any of it. My mind raced to the scene in my dorm room just a few minutes earlier. I heard God's voice. He spoke to me! But, just like the Bible, he was so confusing. Why would he tell me to follow him? Did I mess up? Was I supposed to follow him forward and somehow made myself shoot backward from fear of going to hell? How could I follow him now only to be looking at death once again? And, what was I even dying from?!

The operating room was large, very sterile, and very white. My energy level was slipping fast. Once again, I wanted to go to sleep. A plump Anesthesiologist walked over to me. She was very gentle and kind. She raised her small white hand above my head.

"Sweetie, I'm going to place this over your face, okay?" She positioned the contraption over my nose as she spoke. "I need you to count backward slowly from ten?"

I nodded. She walked over to her station as I began the backward descent.

"Ten…nine…eight…seven…six…"

I blacked out.

A SECOND CHANCE

"**M**s. Bell..."
    I felt someone gently shake me. I looked around to see several unfamiliar faces in my surroundings. I felt discombobulated and pretty sore.

"You're in recovery."

I stared in the smiling face of Dr. Klein.

"Everything went really well. We're going to get you to your room?" She warmly beamed.

"Ok," I slowly nodded.

I was whizzed down even more corridors. It was very confusing considering I was in the neonatal unit of the hospital. Plus, I felt terribly alone and didn't even know if my family had been contacted. Worse yet, I wasn't sure if anyone knew how to even get in contact with them. I didn't want to ask all of these questions rushing through my head. But, the biggest one of all was what in the world happened?!

A sweet mahogany complexioned nurse, with a slender frame and dark chestnut eyes, wheeled me into a private room. She gently assisted me from my wheelchair onto a ready-made bed. Moments later, the doctor returned. Given the chain of events, I knew the information she needed to share was going to be intense. But, I had no idea the news that followed would require someone skilled enough to maneuver a small forklift into my hospital room to lift my jaw off the ground. Dr. Klein dropped the stats like an atomic bomb.

"Your situation was pretty critical." She stared directly into my eyes.

"What happened?" I braced myself for the news.

"You experienced an ectopic pregnancy."

"A what?!" I shrieked.

"An ectopic pregnancy." Dr. Klein stated evenly a second time. "After assessing your symptoms and not finding anything on the monitor, once you said abortion, I knew we literally only had minutes to save your life."

"But, how could I still be pregnant?!" I stammered. "I had an abortion."

"But, there was no baby in your uterus." Dr. Klein gently shook her head. "The fetus attached itself to your fallopian tube. And as the baby began to grow, your tube wasn't able to support the expansion."

"So, what happened?" My mind raced in circles.

"Your fallopian tube ruptured causing severe internal bleeding." She slowly crossed her arms. "My medical team had to promptly perform the emergency surgery to remove your right fallopian tube and stop the bleeding.

"What?!" I shrieked.

"We had no other choice." She shook her head. "We also had to administer a blood transfusion since you lost two liters of blood."

I sat on the bed completely numb, shocked, and confused. I couldn't believe what I was hearing. I was mortified, angry, and bewildered beyond belief. But, after speaking to the doctor in-depth, all the missing pieces were patched together and slowly started making sense. Turns out, the abortion clinic that I visited in Detroit a few weeks earlier totally butchered my insides and did not complete the procedure correctly. Dr. Sanjay executed the abortion all the while knowing there was no fetus in my uterus. Instead of halting the process and recommending I seek emergency help, he proceeded anyway. I sat on the bed internally seething upon hearing the news. Now, it made sense as I reflected why Dr. Sanjay kept prodding away with the ultrasound and nothing appeared on the screen. And, it further justified the reason he became irritated when I questioned whether he saw a baby. I thought back to how he never gave a response. Only a deliberate, "let's get started." I sat in utter disbelief. *How inhumane! How unethical! How evil!* I wanted to scream at the top of my lungs out of anger, pain, and shame. But, I couldn't. Not even if I wanted to. My body was still recovering and seriously sore. I could only momentarily process the information just revealed and do everything in my power to choke back tears. I stared into the compassionate face of Dr. Klein.

"So, you're telling me, if that doctor would've admitted that something looked strange, none of this would've happened?" I uttered through the thick lump rising in the back of my throat.

"Yes." she regretfully nodded. "At least you would've caught the ectopic pregnancy early enough before the fetus ruptured your fallopian tube.

"I can't believe this is happening to me," I sobbed.

"I'm sorry." Dr. Klein's emotions surfaced softening her professional demeanor.

I sat in that hospital bed completely horrified. *How could* *someone who touted himself as a medical professional perform such a callous procedure? Why would he do this to me? Was $250 really worth causing me to potentially lose my life?* Tears flowed down my face. I failed to comprehend the moral rationale in any of it.

"You're very lucky to be alive." Dr. Klein interrupted my thoughts.

"I know," I nodded processing the weight of her words. "Thank you." I sniffed as a tear rolled down my cheek.

"You should be thanking your roommate." She directly affirmed.

"Why…" I wiped my eye.

"Had she not acted as quickly as she did, you would've been dead within sixty minutes."

Those last words hit like a ton of bricks! She was right. Lil D was truly a lifesaver. While I mentally processed everything that just occurred, the medical team who performed my surgery began filing in the small space. I was tremendously grateful for their skill, intelligence, and expertise. I was also appreciative of the paramedic team. If they hadn't followed their own gut intuition in taking me to the emergency OB-GYN ward instead of listening to my nonsense about not being pregnant, I would've died. The emotions engulfing me were overwhelming. I tearfully thanked all of the doctors for their dedication in saving my life. I was so grateful to God for blessing me with such an advanced, skilled, and compassionate medical team. I guess my sister was wrong. Not everyone dies at Grady Hospital. The staff at Grady actually saved my life! Matter of fact, I was shocked to discover the team consisted of very young intern doctors who were responsible for my care.

I learned within that moment that God was still with me. He wasn't mad like I thought. And, he didn't hate me after having the abortion. I cried tears of regret, sadness, relief, and joy. Oh, how I cried. I cried a river. I realized that God had given me a second chance to get my life right. I didn't deserve it. But, Jesus and my heavenly Father granted me grace anyhow. I never understood the four words God spoke to me at the time of my first death when he said, *"Follow me my daughter."* But, a very powerful scripture in John 16:1 (NIV) says, "All this I have told you so that you will not go astray." Clearly, I was on a one-way path to hell! Even in my mishaps and disobedience, God still had mercy on me. He still forgave me. And, he was determined to help, guide, and direct my steps even now. It took death, to halt me in my tracks and out of my unscrupulous ways to understand the importance of changing my life. There were so many pieces of the puzzle to pick up. I had to do it one by one.

THE TONE OF FORGIVENESS

The hospital contacted the college, who in turn contacted my mother and father. Needless to say, they were hysterical! A stream of questions flowed like raging waters. My worst fear came to light a second time. Initially, I hoped to never share the abortion with anyone. Now, it seemed everyone was slowly discovering my dark morbid truth. The bible states in St. Luke 8:17 (KJV), "For nothing is secret, that shall not be made manifest, neither anything hid, that shall not be made known." That scripture spoke volumes and was right. All of my business was coming to light! I spoke to my mother and father for hours on the telephone in the hospital. Both were grateful for the medical staff saving my life. My mother made plans to immediately leave Detroit to be with me. My poor sister was a hot mess after processing everything that occurred. She definitely took the news the hardest and felt somewhat responsible for this tragedy considering she placed me in touch with Sabrina who in turn told me about the abortion clinic. But, it wasn't my sister's fault. I felt terrible that she blamed herself.

Later that evening, after the smoke cleared, I laid awake in bed pondering profusely over the circumstances that led to my death. I tried to make sense out of everything. But, it was difficult. I was still traumatized at how Dr. Sanjay cruelly botched my insides without a care in the world. He was only concerned about working for the almighty dollar at any cost. I felt helpless and overwhelmed. The more I thought about the heartless demented operations within that clinic, the more nauseous I became. I tried to allow my thoughts to drift away from Dr. Sanjay. But instead of finding solace in the stillness of the hospital room, I only found more distress. I wondered what would happen once I left? How long would it take for me to completely heal? Would I ever heal emotionally from this horrid ordeal? I wished that I could focus on something more positive and tried to center my attention on how grateful I was to be alive. I even closed my eyes to re-envision play by play everything that occurred. I quietly reflected on the miraculous experience I encountered just hours earlier. A bewildered smile smeared across my lips as I mentally immersed into that amazing journey. It was exhilarating to know there was definitely another place beyond this earthly realm. For so long I doubted it. Now, I knew it was true! And, it was amazing to attest that I felt absolutely zero pain during my transcendence through the afterlife. But, most incredible yet, I took a deep breath as I cherished the most prevailing part. The memory that sent chills down my spine. I came face-to-face with God. Not only did he stop me dead in my tracks, but he spoke to me. I heard his voice! That was phenomenal! I sat back and slowly exhaled. I experienced all of this wonderment. But, I still sat confused. Everything happened so fast. *Why didn't God tell me more?* I wondered. *Why didn't he take me further into the afterlife? Why didn't he just take my spirit with him then?* I knew there had to be more expected considering I was still alive. The thought of the unknown made my temples throb. *Why did God allow me to die only to force me back into this same body and this identical life? What was I supposed to do?!* I pondered intently. God knew I was living my life fancy-free and doing me. I totally didn't fit the bill of an ideal Christian. So, why did he choose me? I wished God had spoken more. But, he shot me back. There were so many questions burning deep inside. Now, I stood in an even more precarious position. The blasphemous sinner now turned true believer. Who could I share my experience with, and they not assume I was totally insane! What was I supposed to do?

The next couple of days were the same. I experienced pain and more pain. As the night lingered and the silence thickened, I lay in bed severely sore. I slowly inhaled and exhaled recalling the ice-cold breeze in the afterlife and remembered the soothing eradication of pain. But now things were different. Throbbing engulfed my lower abdomen and the pain was pure hell. I gazed upon my stomach all tattered and bruised. There were incisions here, tubes there, and bandages holding me down. Mentally, I found myself slipping down a slippery slope. I couldn't help but wonder what Winston was doing at that moment? Was he even thinking about me? Did he ever call my house in Detroit to make sure I was ok? As much as I wanted to find an excuse, I knew there was none. Especially considering my mother confirmed in our conversation earlier that morning he hadn't called. My blood boiled and my temper ignited. I suddenly felt stupid and used. *Why did this happen to me? Why didn't Winston have to suffer?!* I wrestled over and over with the reality of being confined to a hospital bed. I looked around the cold drab room and fumed. *Why was I the one 800 miles away from home going through hell?* The more I pondered the angrier I became. Especially considering I was immensely sore and couldn't even carry out a simple everyday task like walking. At that moment, I gazed down at my stomach to realize that my once tightly toned abs now encompassed disgusting silver staples that pinched the lower walls. Plus, there was a nasty clear secretion oozing through the gauze bandage at every turn. I was disgusted! My body hurt like Hades. And, it was all Winston's fault! A commanding verse in the bible, Jeremiah 18:15 (KJV) states, "Because my people hath forgotten me, they have burned incense to vanity." I was no different. I should've been ashamed of myself. Here I was just delivered from the grave. But, instead of paying homage to God who saved and delivered me from death, I focused on my compromised figure instead. I should have been singing praises to Jesus' precious name. But, I stared at the ceiling and reflected on my ratchet ex-boyfriend instead. I was lonely in that hospital room. And, the thought of Winston made me even lonelier. His lack of concern sent me reeling! Out of angst, pain, and rage, I found myself reaching for the telephone cradled next to my bed. *Why should he get to comfortably live his life in Detroit while I'm down here suffering?!* Wincing through soreness and struggling at every turn, I managed to pick up the handset and dial Winston's number. I wasn't sure what I was going to say. I just knew I was tired of feeling mentally, physically, and emotionally compromised. It's time he felt the same. The ringing stopped.

"Hello," Winston casually breathed on the other end.

"I can't believe you never called me!" I screamed.

"What?!" He stumbled.

"You heard me!"

"Hold up..." He bellowed. "Who is this even calling me from an out of state number?!"

"Tee!" I shrieked.

"How was I supposed to call you..." He stammered. "I didn't even know where you were?!"

"Atlanta!" I yelled. "The same place where your baby almost killed me!"

"Huh?"

"Exactly!" I snapped. "I'm in the hospital!"

"The hospital? What are you talking about?"

"I had to get emergency surgery because of you!" I shouted. "You and this stupid pregnancy!" I broke down in tears.

How was I supposed to know?!" Winston frantically pleaded.

"You didn't even call to check on me!" I sobbed. "You would've known if you called!"

"Tee, please don't cry..."

"You don't care!" I blared through tears. "You never cared!"

"That's not fair!" He insisted. "I didn't know!"

Well, that part could've held some truth. After all, I never called him after I decided to go through with the abortion. Instead, I just vanished from the city without a trace. So, I guess I played my part in the lack of communication production. But, then again, that didn't excuse the fact that Winston and his mother failed to check on me. After all, I was pregnant and in a terrible situation. Winston knew his condom came off. He also knew better than anyone that pregnancy was possible from this mishap. Yet, he never reached out. Not once! So, in the whole scheme of things, it wasn't cool that I was the one lying in a hospital bed.

"Not fair?" I shouted hysterically. "It's not fair I almost died!"

"I'm sorry…" He pleaded. "I swear I didn't know…"

I paused at his last words. This is what I thought I wanted to hear from him. I yearned for acknowledgment, recognition of my suffering, and a sincere apology when I initially called. But, now that Winston just apologized, it didn't make me feel any better. In fact, it made me feel worse. I couldn't believe that I allowed myself to get so worked up in the first place. I could've busted one of my staples. Or, made my blood pressure sharply rise. Yelling, crying, and stressing in my current state was absolutely irrational. I allowed my emotions to get the best of me. I should've focused my energy on the second chance I was given at life. But instead, I lay in bed cradling the phone screaming and acting a fool. Naturally, I was devastated that I hadn't heard from Winston. I wanted to make him hurt too. I wanted him to feel terrible for not being there for me. I guess I succeeded. But, the call still didn't go as planned. I didn't feel better. As I began to wrestle with my wrath, a light knock rapped on the door. I tried to raise myself up on my elbow as the evening nurse shuffled through. I pressed the receiver close to my lips.

"Winston…" I breathed.

"Yeah?" He paused.

"I gotta go.

Before he could utter a single word, I hung up. I felt relief in knowing that at least he now knew what happened to me.

After the evening nurse checked my vitals, she left me all alone with my thoughts. I sat recapping the conversation over and over in my head. *Maybe I was wrong for blaming Winston for the whole fiasco. It wasn't like he held a gun to my head and forced me to have sex.* I realized that I had to take ownership for my part too. But, I still felt a slight sting of rage. I was in a bad place and not at peace. I felt this unrelenting spirit to hold onto blame. A commanding verse in the bible in St. Luke 6:37 (KJV) states, "Judge not, and ye shall not be judged: condemn not, and ye shall not be condemned: forgive, and ye shall be forgiven." I knew God had just forgiven me in a major way! Even after all my recklessness as a teen, God still showed mercy. So, who was I to harbor animosity towards Winston? He gave a sincere apology on the phone. Therefore, I knew I couldn't continue onward carrying hatred, ill will, or malevolence towards him in my heart. For my own sanity, I needed to internally find a way of making amends. To do that, I would have to heal emotionally, physically, and spiritually. Then, I recalled a powerful verse in Ephesians 4:32 (KJV) that says, "And be ye kind one to another, tenderhearted, forgiving one another, even as God for Christ's sake hath forgiven you." The tone of forgiveness kept ringing over and over in my head. I knew it was something that God required of me. This would not be an easy task to execute. I endured so much. Plus, I vowed internally to never speak to Winston from that day forward. But, even if I never talked to Winston again, I desperately needed to find it within my heart to forgive him. Everything wasn't totally his fault. I had to be honest and admit that we both played a part. Bit by bit, I reconciled in my spirit. I needed to find solace to forgive him. I was confident it could be accomplished one day. Maybe with a little time, I could even learn to forgive myself.

MOVING FORWARD

The road to recovery was a difficult one. The most challenging part of the equation was the aftermath that followed. I didn't have health insurance. So, I had to go back to Grady Hospital for my follow up exam since I didn't have a private practitioner. I met with Dr. Price, a middle-aged, friendly-faced, white male gynecologist. He was nice enough. But, the visit was unnerving considering I was accustomed to having female doctors examine me. But, since I didn't have much choice. The visit ensued.

"Your incision is healing very well." Dr. Price pulled down my gown. "We should be able to remove your staples soon."

"Cool," I nodded. "I was scared for a second."

"No need to be." He smiled. "I just recommend you don't overexert yourself."

"I won't."

"Good. So, I'll see you back in another two weeks and we can check your progress."

"Ok." I nodded"

"Any questions for me?" He grabbed his chart.

"Maybe one." I hesitantly bit my lip.

"Go ahead…"

"Well, I know it's early…" I segued. "And, it's not like I plan to do anything anytime soon. But, when I do, will we discuss birth control options later down the line?"

"Birth control? Why?" Dr. Price looked perplexed.

"So I won't get pregnant again." I winced equally confused.

"Oh, you don't have to worry about that." He flipped through his chart.

"Why not?" My mind drew a blank.

"Because according to your records you're not able to have children."

"What?!" I couldn't believe my ears.

"I'm looking at it right here." He scanned notes in the chart.

I felt stuck in the Twilight Zone. As I blankly stared back, Dr. Price informed me of my infertile state. Apparently, the trauma I experienced due to the ruptured fallopian tube and surgery was so severe that it left me barren. I sat completely numb, dazed, and confused. As much as I wanted to scream, I felt this must be the ultimate cost and consequence for my sin. It seemed there were lots of consequences and repercussions due to my actions with Winston. Perhaps, I deserved it. Maybe, this was God's way of teaching me a serious lesson. I tried not to beat myself up about it. I even attempted to find a silver lining woven within this fabric. I tried to focus on the fact that at least I was alive! But, when it rains it pours. And, that old adage began to ring loud and clear.

After the doctor's office dealt a serious blow, the windstorm of life kept propelling. Just as I began to digest the barrenness of my body, I had to cope with the second wave of bad news that affected my college career. My mother had to meet with school administrators after my release from the hospital to decide how to move forward from this ordeal. Naturally, I was still in immense pain and on the journey to recovery. But, I was in no position to weather matriculation on campus or even attend my classes. Worst yet, I couldn't even manage to climb the three flights of stairs leading to my college dorm room. So, the powers that be requested a meeting of the minds to figure the best course of action.

The campus of Clark Atlanta University was bustling with fall semester underway. My mother and I arrived on campus and steadily strolled over to an old red brick administration building that read Harkness Hall. I pulled my baseball cap lower over my head and averted all eye contact tucking my chin deep into my chest. I prayed that I didn't bump into any of my friends and hoped no one in the administration building would recognize me either. Luckily, the coast was clear. The building was actually pretty empty with the exception of a few students lingering by a side stair rail. The hallway was covered in dark wood, shiny tiled floors, and a stillness that exuded prominence and sophistication behind every door. My mother glanced down at her sheet of paper scribbled with notes, room numbers, and names. She abruptly stopped, glanced at her sheet once more, then looked up at the office number on the door. She grabbed the handle and walked directly up to the counter where the receptionist, a fresh-faced spritely young lady sat. The receptionist pressed her red reading glasses closer to her caramel face.

"Good morning mam, may I help you?" The receptionist inquired.

"Yes, my name is Ms. Bell this is my daughter." My mother turned toward me. "We have an appointment with Dean Withers."

"Ok. What is it regarding?" The receptionist pressed.

"She's already aware and awaiting our arrival." My mother sternly shut down any further interrogation.

"Sure thing." The receptionist uneasily grabbed the phone. "I'll let her know you're here. Please have a seat."

I nervously glanced around the office. My mother sat cool as a cucumber. I had no idea what to expect or what my fate might be. But, before I could allow my nerves to get the best of me the door leading to Dean Wither's office slowly opened. Dean Withers, a petite woman, Maxine Waters type, with a slow stride, and seasoned no-nonsense demeanor warmly smiled as she approached wearing a long navy skirt, white blouse, and navy blazer draping her small frame.

"Good morning Ms. Bell." She extended her hand to my mother.

"Good morning." My mother graciously reached for Dean Withers.

"Right this way." Dean Withers motioned.

The Dean's office was quite prestigious and relatively large with multiple recognition plaques, degrees, and Delta paraphernalia cascading the walls. We walked over to her huge cherry wood desk. There were several large books, binders, and papers strewn about.

"It's been such a busy morning." Dean Withers rattled. "Please have a seat." She motioned.

My mother and I politely slid into two cushioned seats across from her desk.

"Thank you for being able to meet with us on such short notice." My mother glanced at the Dean.

"This is a pretty critical situation. So, we want to do all that we can to ensure this young lady is well and can continue her studies." Dean Withers nodded.

"We really appreciate that." My mother replied.

"So how are you feeling?" Dean Withers pivoted my direction.

"I'm still a little sore. But, I feel much better." I nervously responded.

I hated having to speak about my well-being. It was a constant reminder of the reason that I was in such a mess to begin with.

"Well, we're certainly happy that you're feeling much better." Dean Withers smiled. "You gave everyone quite a scare."

"Us back home too." My mother quickly chimed. "And given our telephone conversation Dean Withers, I wanted to discuss how we can proceed forward with her education in light of this recent incident."

Dean Withers momentarily paused. Then calmly cusped her hands together as if to carefully gather her next words.

"Well, as you know we definitely want what's best for our students." Dean Withers glanced in my direction. "But, safety is our primary concern. And, we need to warrant that she will be able to safely pursue her studies given the extreme nature of her condition."

"I understand." My mother crossed her legs. "So, what do you recommend?"

I sat on edge trying to contain the overwhelming sense of

anxiety bubbling in the pit of my stomach. I fixedly stared across the table at the Dean.

"She's going to have to return home for a few months to recuperate." Dean Withers stared intently at my mom. "Given her condition and recent surgery, unfortunately, administration can't risk any liability that may occur with her being on campus. We need her completely healed."

I sighed uneasily. This wasn't quite the news that I wanted to hear. But, I wasn't very shocked at this onslaught of information. Administrators on campus, as well as my family, both feared for my safety considering staples still covered the lower abdomen area where doctors removed the tube. I couldn't risk re-opening the enclosed area from something as simple as a student bumping into me or even climbing stairs. It was just too dangerous. So, the decision was imminent just like my fate.

"But what about her studies?" My mother worriedly fired. "Would she still be able to graduate on time if she left?"

"Well," the Dean paused. "We did consider one possibility to keep her on target."

"Which is…" My mother skeptically questioned.

"If she's able to stay in line with her studies in Michigan," Dean Withers paused. "We can speak to her instructors and have them provide all coursework for the rest of the semester."

"That would be great!" I perked up.

"But, young lady…" Dean Withers stared directly at me. "You would be responsible for completing and returning all coursework in a timely fashion."

"I will keep up!" I chimed.

"You sure?" Dean Withers raised a brow. "It will require a

lot of work, dedication, and focus. No one will be in Michigan to assist you."

Although I had no idea how to home school myself, I was prepared to do whatever necessary to graduate on time. "Yes!" I convincingly nodded. "I've been on the honor roll my entire life. I catch on quickly. I can do it."

"Ok," Dean Withers tilted her head. "That will be your responsibility."

"I promise I won't let you down." I beamed.

"I believe you." She smiled. "I see the drive in your eyes. And, we're here to support you."

"Thanks so much." I nodded.

I had to admit, this was awesome news in the midst of a terrible ordeal. At least I was given an opportunity to stay in line with my studies from afar and I would be allowed to return to school at the beginning of winter semester. Maybe things were starting to turn around after all.

"So, looks like we're all in agreement here." Dean Withers glanced at my mother.

"Yes," My mother nodded.

"Great." Dean Withers motioned to stand.

"But, wait!" I sat upright.

"Everything ok?" Dean Withers grew concerned.

"I just remembered." I hesitated. "What about me leaving the dorm?"

My mother reading my worried expression chimed in.

"Will anyone know what happened to her?" She interrupted. "This is such a personal matter."

"No need to worry Ms. Bell", Dean Weathers folded her arms. "Administrators, professors, the Resident Advisor, and even her roommate will be held to a strict code of silence."

"Which means?" My mother raised a brow.

"No one will know." The Dean assured. "They are not allowed to discuss anything with anyone."

"Thank you." My mother uttered just above a whisper.

That was a huge relief considering it was my biggest fear. I couldn't stomach the gossip or fake news that could potentially ensue with my disappearance. So at least for now, it looked like my devastating tragedy would be held in the strictest of confidentiality. Out of all of the bad news that I had to bear, this made me feel slightly better. But even though everyone was sworn to secrecy, I still couldn't fathom how to explain to friends on campus where did I go for so long? Even my cousin Nikki was clueless as to the real ordeal. Her dorm was adjacent to mine and we rarely interacted at all during Freshmen Week. I wondered if she even knew.

THE JOURNEY HOME

The long journey home was a somber one. Mentally, I was consumed with grief. The realization of being barren, the apprehension of leaving school, and the uncertainty of the future was a hard pill to digest. On one hand, I was exuberant to be alive. Yet on the other, I felt shattered to pick up the pieces by having to explain how my life almost ended. How would I begin to explain this travesty? Surely, questions would mount north, south, east, and west. My friends on campus would want to know why I left school. My friends in Detroit would want to know why I returned home. My family would be curious for answers as well. And for once, I was speechless. But, after much contemplation, I thought maybe it would be best to just be honest and tell the truth. Perhaps, I should just put it out there and come clean. But, surprisingly my mother was adamantly against it. At first, I was shocked. I couldn't understand why she didn't support my decision. But, then it hit me. I never took her image into consideration. My family was a really traditional, super old school, and church meant everything to my mother.

My inner demons had the potential to shatter her joy, pride, and reputation within intimate church circles. For once, my mother was really able to brag. She was a single mother with three children, two of which were in college. It wouldn't be a good look to disclose that one of them made a mistake. A huge mistake! That I had gotten pregnant and almost died in school. That would bring nothing but embarrassment and shame to my family. So, my mother thought it best not to disclose the full story. Instead, she strategically instructed me to tell everyone that I had Appendicitis. I was basically advised to say that my appendix ruptured while I was asleep. That would answer any question that came my way considering an appendix needed to be surgically removed if an unexpected infection occurred. Luckily in my situation, it was believable. Even down to the surgical scarring. No one would refute this story.

It looked like my family had forgiven me. Lips in my immediate clan were sealed and my secret was safe once again. Up until this point, only my mother, father, sister, grandmother, and grandfather were aware. No one would utter one word. This manufactured story covered the surface scar. But, like fabricating anything goes, it left a deeper scar of spiritual confusion. Now, how could I ever share my near-death experience? How could I reveal to anyone that I heard God's voice? How would I be able to share any part of my spiritual journey if the true undertaking was now tangled with a lie? The Bible states in Colossians, 3:9-10 (KJV) "Lie not one to another, seeing that ye have put off the old man with his deeds; And have put on the new man, which is renewed in knowledge after the image of him that created him." This verse spoke volumes. But, I didn't have enough courage to bear my cross publicly. Besides, I couldn't. I wasn't prepared to share the whole truth. And at the same time, I wasn't about to share the details of my near-death experience and muddle it with a lie.

The only person that I told I heard God's voice was my mother. She instantly believed me. But, neither of us was sure what to do with the experience. Not to mention, my family still had its dignity and image to bear. So with that said the true divine gift of knowing there was a God, the presence of an afterlife, and the fact that I heard God's voice would just have to be between me and God. I thought that's what God wanted. So, I decided I would do what God told me to do. I would follow him. But, I would do it quietly. I would change my ways. And, I would acknowledge his existence. I would go to church. I would openly do better, be better, and renounce my old anti-religious ways. I thought this was good enough for God. My soul was going to be saved and I was going to do right going forward in God's sight. Perhaps the words that he spoke and the message implied were only for me. Boy was I wrong.

AN APPOINTED TIME

It's amazing how your life, deeds, and your actions whether good or bad have the power to transcend and touch the lives of others around you. As time progressed, more things were revealed to me following my near-death experience. I discovered that I wasn't the only one affected by the trauma. Once I returned to school, I learned Lil D had to take a leave of absence as well. It turned out, the stress that she experienced from that horrific night was just too difficult to bear.

Goosebumps covered my arms as I opened the door to our dorm room. It felt strange knowing I wouldn't have Lil D by my side to share secrets, laughs, eat at the dining hall, or peruse the campus. I felt really guilty. I hadn't spoken to her since the ordeal. Both of our parent's finances were ill stretched. So, we didn't have the luxury of calling long distance non-stop. But, I needed to talk to Lil D. It just didn't feel right being back in the A-T-L with Lil D not in school. I needed to know that she was ok. I would just have to eat this bill. I picked up the phone.

"Hello…" a familiar voice rang on the other end.

"Hey Lil D!"

"What's up Tee?!" She squealed. "How are you?"

"A lot better." I beamed. "What's up with you?"

"Taking a break." She paused. "But, I'll be back next semester in the fall."

"That's good." I crossed my legs on the bed. "Girl, nobody even told me you went back home."

"I had too." She sighed. "It was just too much."

"Yeah, things did get crazy down here." I glanced around the room.

"Tell me about it." Lil D exhaled. "I still can't believe you almost died!"

"I hate thinking about it." I shook my head.

"Girl, you scared the mess out of me! It was like something out of a horror movie."

"I know…" I breathed.

"I'm still trippin' you just sat on the bed with this weird look on your face."

"Like what?"

"I don't know. It was just weird. Like blank." She paused. "I kept screaming your name. But, you just stared back not saying nothing."

"I remember…"

"But then, your eyes turned white and rolled to the back of your head!"

"What?" I shrieked.

"Girl yes!" Her voice elevated. "You literally passed out and fell backwards on the bed."

"Are you serious?!"

"As a heart attack!" Lil D exclaimed. "I ran out of that room as fast as I could to get help. It totally freaked me out!"

It was one thing to experience that night first hand. But, it was another to hear Lil D's recap. I had no idea my body went into shock like that.

"That's crazy! I would've freaked too."

"Girl, I couldn't stay in that room afterwards." Lil D continued. "I had nightmares all the time. It was just too much."

"Dang," the weight of her words hit me. "That's real messed up."

I glanced around Lil D's side of the room. It was just as barren as my insides and vacant as the day I strolled through the door Freshman Week. Only now, it felt smaller and more desolate without her here.

"D, I'm really sorry you had to go through this."

"I know." She sighed. "I'm just happy you're alive."

"Me too," I exhaled.

It was truly a blessing to have Lil D in my life. I don't know what I would've done without her. I sat and thought about Lil D for a long time. It amazed me how God orchestrated our friendship and knew first-hand how everything would go down. God knew the minute that I received my acceptance letter to Clark Atlanta University that Lil D would be my roommate. Just like he knew within the first sixty seconds that we met she would save my life a few days later. God made sure that I had a roommate that I bonded with and someone who cared enough to rise up in the middle of the night and act in haste. That same scenario would've been devastating had it been different. If Lil D and I met for the first time and hated one another, the end result could've proven fatal. She could have awakened, seen me struggling, heard me say I had to throw up, and simply thought, "She'll be alright." I could have literally died. Instead, God knew it was critical that we became friends. It was imperative that he placed someone in my life that had the qualities of being compassionate, calm, and quick to act.

The more I sat and reflected, the more I found it unfathomable how sins I committed in Michigan followed me down to Georgia just to wreak havoc on another girl's life. But, it goes to show that no one understands God's plan. Or, why he places people in our lives at the moment that he does. I regretted wholeheartedly that Lil D had to experience such torment. But, I understood it was necessary. Lil D was a pivotal factor in saving my life. Had she not been my roommate, I would have died. The same thing can be said for the medical team who arrived on the scene at my dorm. They totally ignored my pleas and acted within their own intuition. That was a blessing. I definitely can't leave out the doctor in the emergency room. She only heard four words "I had an abortion" and knew exactly what to do. I sometimes wondered what would have happened if the doctor had been wrong. What if I didn't suffer an ectopic pregnancy? I only mentioned that I had an abortion. I never shared anything regarding the procedure. But, her first response was, "We must go to surgery now". I'm thankful to God she was knowledgeable, intuitive, and spot on! It was obvious that God placed her in my life at that moment for an appointed time.

That's when it hit me. God really does have the ultimate plan in hand. We are absolutely oblivious to this factor. But, God's power is so paramount that he places people in your life five days down the line, five months down the line, even five, and fifteen, and fifty years down the line who will be the biggest blessing to you. Before this incident, I failed to give God credit for his omnipotence and relationship that he had with me. An arresting verse in Jeremiah 1:5 (KJV) states, "Before I formed thee in the belly I knew thee…" This verse alone signifies that God knew me very well before my feet ever touched the ground in this earthly realm. I was so grateful to God for his love, his mercy, and for the people that he placed in my life for an appointed time. I was so grateful for this breakthrough. I wanted to learn more and I yearned to build a closer relationship with him. I needed to gain a better understanding of the purpose that God had in store for my life.

REVELATION

Things were being revealed to me so swiftly that my inner discernment could barely keep up. I wanted to comprehend what to do with all of this new understanding. During college, God kept me from falling numerous times. As a result, my bond thickened with him beyond belief. I can definitely confess from the moment that I nearly died, heard his voice, and was given a second chance that I never doubted his existence ever again. I attended church regularly. I became more vocal about the goodness of God. And surprisingly a few years after my near-death experience, I was blessed with a child in spite of what doctors said, one fallopian tube and all! It goes to show that God works in his own timing. He will show up and show out just to reveal his wonders. A very powerful scripture in the bible, St. Mark 10:27 (KJV) states, "With men it is impossible, but not with God: for with God all things are possible." That scripture spoke volumes and utter truth for my life. God's great authority fascinated me. And, I wanted so desperately to share. But, I was caught in a quandary. Everyone in my family and my close circle of friends still thought that I had my appendix removed. I wasn't quite sure how to dispel this lie. Initially, I began to minister to individuals one on one to share the goodness of God. I would even encounter non-believers whereby I'd strike up a conversation and simply end it with, believe me I know there's a God. I almost died. But, I would just leave it at that.

Years later, I received a revelation while speaking with my boyfriend Nasir. He was incredibly attractive with deep expresso skin, sunken cheeks, and slanted coal eyes. Nasir grew up in Sierra Leone and experienced abandonment at a very early age when his mother split after his parent's divorce. He was unsure about how to establish relationships. He often shared that his childhood was filled with tremendous turmoil and abuse. Nasir couldn't understand why God would allow children to experience such pain. Not to mention, his adulthood was equally tumultuous and he continued to question God. I was determined to change his outlook. To the point, I haphazardly shared my near-death experience leaving out critical details surrounding the abortion and such. I simply disclosed to him that I died and heard the voice of God. I didn't reveal exactly what God said. I just wanted him to grasp the foremost fact that God existed. Needless to say, Nasir was shocked.

"You are so selfish!" He shouted.

"What?!" That definitely wasn't the reaction I expected.

"How can you go through something like that and not tell anyone?"

"Because…" I stammered.

"Because why?!" He fumed.

"I'm just not ready." I exhaled.

"Really Tee?" He raised a brow.

"Well, I'm not." I turned from his heated gaze.

"Tee, God blessed you with that experience! And, you're just going to keep it all to yourself?" He winced.

I was totally caught off guard. Why was he so upset? Why was he attacking me?

"Well, maybe he did it so I could turn my life around!" I exploded.

"Or, maybe he wanted you to share it with everybody else!" He snapped back. "Did you ever stop to think about that?"

Suddenly, we both grew silent. I had to admit Nasir made a valid point. I let out a deep sigh and stared at the floor. My thoughts were totally consumed.

"I'm just saying," he interrupted my thoughts. "Maybe you're supposed to share that experience with as many non-believers as possible?"

"What?" I frowned.

"It could be what God wants you to do. Maybe that's your purpose."

"I'm not so sure about that." I breathed.

"Well, I am." He moved closer to me.

"Nasir…"

"I'm telling you." He placed his hand over mine. "You have a sense of realness about you Tee. People will listen to you because you sinned just like everybody else."

"It's just too much." I heaved. "I'm not ready."

I tried to hold my ground. But, deep down inside, I knew Nasir was right. It's crazy that once I realized this critical fact I never followed up on my mission. I didn't even attempt to share my testimony. Nasir and I broke up a few months later.

And although we were no longer a couple, his words stayed with me. I heard them clear as day. They played over and over in my head. Nonetheless, I didn't attempt to reach the masses. I was too afraid. So, I simply continued to speak sparingly to individuals one on one. After all, I figured talking to a few people was better than none. I tried to create my own plan. I began to minister to a few ex-boyfriends sharing my watered-down testimony. Watered down meaning all of the circumstances leading to my near-death experience minus the abortion. I contrived in my head a ridiculous notion that perhaps God wanted me to utilize my womanly wiles to bring men to the kingdom. It was easier to talk to a wayward boyfriend then the multitudes. Plus, I was somewhat successful in getting them to go to church and recognize God's existence. But, God still expected more. The way I was carrying out this mission was not pleasing in his sight. The old adage goes, "when you know better you do better". But, I fell short. To a certain degree, I was taking a short cut in serving as a living testimony. I was living a partial Christian lifestyle. I did the bare minimum in my walk. I was the type of Christian who didn't participate in church activities. But, I would listen to the sermon and tithed sporadically. Then afterwards, I would go about the week doing my regular secular routine.

Surprisingly enough, even though I lived this halfhearted Christian walk, God still remained faithfully by my side. He blessed me with a lucrative job. I stayed in an awesome area in Atlanta, plus as mentioned previously I was blessed with a beautiful daughter and she attended a distinguished school in the city. Things were actually great given I wasn't holding up to my end of the bargain wholeheartedly. This is when I learned that God is truly patient with his children. But, don't get it twisted. His patience only lasts for so long. And, his tolerance started to wear super thin with my shenanigans. God pressed the weight of the world so tough on my shoulders that it seemed everything turned upside down overnight. No matter what I placed my hand upon it fell apart. In 2012, everything hit the fan in a major way. I suddenly developed a fatal food allergy that was previously non-existent. Numerous trips to the doctor made me miss multiple days at work. Instead of receiving compassion from my employer, they terminated me instead. Needless to say, I was distraught! On top of the severe food allergy, I began to experience difficulties breathing. This was unusual for a person who ate well, exercised daily, and had no history of asthma. But, like clockwork, every morning I arose it felt like a 400-pound person straddled my chest. Initially, I thought it was anxiety. But, my daughter developed nosebleeds, dizzy spells, and terrible headaches. It seemed like we were cursed. Doctors were clueless to our symptoms no matter how many tests were conducted. All of them produced zero results. I racked my brain for answers. The only thought I could settle on was there must be something wrong with the house. As crazy as it sounded, we felt like hell in the house. However, our symptoms disappeared whenever we left. I remembered when I worked for a mold attorney many of our clients had bizarre intermittent symptoms as well. I contacted an air quality inspector that my previous firm utilized to test my home. Lord, if life couldn't get any worse, the test results revealed there was toxic black mold throughout my entire home! It was in the walls, under the floors, and under the crawl space of the entire condo. The levels were so extreme I was informed that I would have to vacate immediately and leave all of my belongings behind. With no feasible income infusing into my household, no job, and now no place to live, I was faced with temporary homelessness. My life was in a total whirlwind. I was distraught! I cried night after night why was this happening to me? How did every possible area imaginable in my life fall apart? I was extremely depressed. But, there wasn't enough Xanax to mask the pain. I felt downright suicidal at times. However, I feared taking my life, as I already knew God would be waiting on the other side with some serious consequences to bear. So, I racked my brain trying to figure out a way to create a better situation. Luckily, I managed to secure a temp job. Then, I scraped my last funds together and pleaded to an apartment community to allow me to move in. Thankfully, I found a management team with a heart. That was a blessing in itself considering my credit was busted beyond belief.

As I moved into my unit, I realized my life had truly hit rock bottom. Before, my daughter and I were living the lap of luxury. Now, we slept uncomfortably on air mattresses on the floor. I didn't have any other furniture to fill my barren home. Plus, I wasn't sure how I was going to replace all of our belongings on a temp budget. I barely had enough money to pay rent and buy food. I wanted to die! Why did God save me for this? I prayed feverishly for an answer. I felt really empty and did not know what to do. I read a commanding verse in Habakkuk 2:3 (NIV) which says, "For the revelation awaits an appointed time... though it linger, wait for it; it will certainly come and will not delay."

By fall, I received a call from my best friend, Rick. He was every girl's dream: tall, dark, handsome, and incredibly accomplished. We dated a few years prior. But, it didn't work out. We realized a romance wasn't in the stars and we were best suited as friends. Like most girls, I was very immature when he and I dated early on in our twenties. I didn't realize I had a great man until he was gone. But, thankfully, our love was paramount and we remained steadfast fixtures in each other's lives throughout the years although our romantic relationship fizzled. I admired Rick tremendously and trusted his advice wholeheartedly since he was quite successful. Rick was a very humble and spiritual man. He encompassed characteristics that totally contradicted stereotypes thrown upon athletes. Rick was an incredible support system. He stood by my side through many trials and tribulations and I felt comfortable enough to share my near-death experience with him. Rick was also the only person outside of my immediate family nucleus who was aware of the pregnancy and abortion. I really loved Rick and truly valued his opinion. He was non-judgmental. He was very sweet. And, more importantly, he was my spiritual partner. Whenever either of us had issues going on in our lives, we would call on the other for prayer. It was during this darkest hour that I received his call. I was at my wit's end. It seemed everything in my life had gone to hell in a hand-basket. But, I was too prideful to disclose the real ordeal to my family and friends. I refused to ask for money. Yet, I was drowning in debt and unsure how to get out of this sinking ship. It seemed Rick always had a knack for calling just at the right time. It didn't matter if we hadn't spoken in weeks or sometimes months. He would call at the precise moment that I needed to vent, cry, or pray.

I held the phone crying my eyes out. I wasn't sure how I was going to make it through and I refused to ask Rick for money. But, given he wasn't hurting for funds, I was certain he would offer as he had done in the past.

"You're not going to like what I have to tell you." He paused.

"Nothing would surprise me at this point." I sniffed. "I don't think anything can be worse than what I'm going through."

"Just hear me out." He hesitated.

"I'm listening." I wiped my eyes.

"You know how it seems you always have these extreme moments in your life?"

"Yeah…" I hesitated unsure where this was headed.

"Whenever I talk to you, it always seems like something crazy is going on." He continued.

"And…" I paused.

"And, I'm telling you." He lingered. "Your life is not going to get better until you write that book."

"What?!" I shrieked.

"God wants you to live a life of holiness. He wants you to tell people about your experience."

This was definitely not what I wanted to hear. I took a deep breath and sighed.

"Tee, you have a mission and purpose you're not fulfilling." Rick continued.

"Well…" I stammered.

"I'm telling you," he interrupted. "You're never going to reach that next level in your life until you share your testimony."

"I have a lot going on right now." I snapped.

"Well, I have a feeling more bad things are going to happen until you walk in your purpose."

The phone grew silent. I could not believe Rick was pulpit preaching instead of offering money to help me out of this situation. Low key I was pissed! But, as much as I wanted to find fault with him, deep down inside, I knew he was right. Rick didn't offer to help with my finances. But, he was dropping spiritual words of wisdom to help save my soul. I should have considered that. It was pretty major. But, I got off the phone in a huff instead.

Needless to say, I didn't write the book. And as fate would have it, Rick's words came to fruition. Things kept getting increasingly worse in my life. The Bible says in Deuteronomy 8:5 (NIV), "Know then in your heart that as a man disciplines his son, so the Lord your God disciplines you." And, I was getting my butt spanked by the Lord in the worst kind of way. I kept feeling the heat over and over again. God was not letting up. No matter what I did, nothing in my life was going right. That's what God will do when he has a special covering on your life. When you are out of alignment with God's will, you will feel it. You will have no rest and no peace. Romans 12:2 (KJV) says, "And be not conformed to this world: but be ye transformed by the renewing of your mind, that ye may prove what is good, and acceptable and perfect". It was paramount that I could no longer compress God's will another minute. I wanted to be obedient and oblige to the path he set for me. I knew I had to. But, I was so afraid. I wasn't sure how.

IT'S NEVER EASY WALKING IN TRUTH

My biggest challenge was trying to decide how to carry out the will of God. It was very difficult considering I had kept his revelation a secret for so long? In my contemplation, I found myself realizing how similar I was to the prophet Jonah in the Bible. We shared so many parallels. Jonah was given a purpose to fulfill by God. But, he didn't want to fulfill it either. Matter of fact, he blatantly fled and tried to run away from God so that he would not have to carry it out. But, Jonah's rebellion placed thousands of people's souls at risk because he didn't take God's message of repentance and deliverance to them. And, God made Jonah suffer. This made me quickly realize that God does not play! He never has and he never will. When God has a calling on your life, you can't just flee from it and forget it. It's not that simple. You have to stand firm, ten toes flat, and do what God called you to do. Jonah didn't do this. As a result, his escape was unsuccessful. God caused Jonah to be thrown overboard from a ship and swallowed by a whale. It was in the belly of this fish that Jonah feverishly prayed. God heard Jonah's prayer and had mercy on him. And, God decided to save Jonah. This showed me that no matter what your circumstance is, if you pray from the heart, God will save you. But, don't get it twisted. Just because God grants mercy it doesn't mean he will let you abort the mission. The problem is, as humans, we don't like to tackle and face tribulations. We don't want to deal with anything that is too difficult or uncomfortable. So, to avoid these things like Jonah, we run. Now, you may not board a boat or fall overboard and get swallowed by a whale. But, you may run to different life situations. You may run to a job for security. You might run to alcohol to alleviate the pain. You run to sex for instant gratification. You run to an abusive relationship for love. In essence, you and I have been guilty time and time again of running to the wrong places to escape our purpose and to create what we think is peace, happiness, and joy. But, when we submerge into these vices, we are confronted with a greater calamity of sorts. Then, like Jonah we try to pray our way out. The reality is when you run from your purpose you will find yourself in a mountain of a mess that only God can save you from. In these troubling times, you must humble yourself and pray for deliverance. And, God will save you. But, he still wants you to carry out his will. You can never escape your purpose. After God made Jonah suffer for a while, the Bible says in Jonah 3:1-2 (KJV), "And the word of the Lord came unto Jonah the second time saying, Arise, go unto Nineveh…and preach unto it the preaching that I bid thee." This scripture gave me hope. It blatantly showed even though Jonah was disobedient; God still gave him a second chance to carry out his mission. This meant if God gave Jonah a second chance, he would give me a second chance. And, he would give you one too! It is important to understand that prayer and obedience is key. I already knew if

I humbled myself and prayed I would be forgiven. But, when God forgives you, he still expects you to learn from your mistakes and jump back on the right path. Most times, we fail to follow God because we feel the responsibility is too much to bear. As a result, we prance around our purpose. We try to find cavalier ways to partially do it. But, it's important to understand that you will never experience total fulfillment in your life until you completely carry out God's will for your life. You must walk in your purpose. Please realize there are no short cuts to the kingdom of heaven. Matter of fact you really only have two choices. You can carry out God's purpose for your life. Or, you can decide not to do it. It's really that simple. Let's be clear, God spoke through Nasir the first time to try and convince me to share my testimony. But, I ignored it. So, God made my life immensely uncomfortable and spoke through Rick a second time with a very clear message, "You are not going to reach that next level in your life until you write that book." But, as you know, it's never easy walking in truth, especially when you've been living a lie for so long.

∾

On the Fourth of July, my daughter, sister, brother, mother, and I piled into a car in Atlanta and drove all the way to Ohio to visit our family in Cleveland. We annually made this trek to attend the big Fourth of July party at my cousin Nikki's house. As usual, we were sitting around the table fellowshipping with the cousins, laughing and talking. Typically, we engage about music of the day, fashion, fads, politics, or family drama. But, this time we were talking college and sports. Suddenly, my cousin Nikki chimed in.

"CAU was the bomb! Remember how much fun we had Tee?!"

"No doubt!" I nodded thinking about the good ole days. "That was real messed up what happened to you though." Nikki sighed.

"What!?" My eyebrow rose not sure where this conversation was headed.

"When your appendix burst." She looked at me quizzically.

"My appendix?" I squinted.

"You don't remember that?" She stared in disbelief.

Oh snap! My mind frantically raced. *She's talking about what happened freshman year.* I scanned my mother and sister's face.

"Oh yeah," I sighed. "That was crazy."

But, it was even crazier that I was still holding onto this lie. Reality dug its ragged teeth into the depths of my spine. And, it still hurt that no one knew. Worst yet, I didn't even have the heart to disclose the truth either. I mean how do you begin a conversation of that magnitude over dinner? I guess in hindsight, it could have been a perfect opportunity to share the trauma that I went through. I could have discussed my near-death experience and confessed how amazing God was to spare my life. Who knows how many souls I might've touched in my own family that day. But, I gazed across the table at my mother and sister's nervous expressions shrinking in shame. Then, to make matters worse, my daughter and little brother were present. So, I had to maintain my family honor. I needed to remain silent. I couldn't reveal the shame. But, therein lies the problem. Too many times in our lives, when we have deep secrets that are held close to our chests, we stay silent when we should be speaking out.

Truth be told, it's never an easy time to walk in truth. While I didn't reveal my testimony at that moment, I knew I couldn't go much longer living a lie. My spirit was bothered. I'm not a perfect person and I was tired of living and acting like I was. I needed to reveal my faults. I needed to share God's love and the mercy he granted me. I wanted people to know and understand God's love, his presence, his divinity, and his realness. God really does exist. It doesn't matter what the naysayer, the hypocrites, the Atheists, nor any of the non-believers say. The Lord is real. And, I heard him! But, there was only one way to admit it. And, in doing so, I would have to air all of my dirty laundry. It was only a matter of time.

FAITHFULLY BY MY SIDE

So many times I privately claimed to God that I would share my testimony with the masses. But, every time I failed out of fear. A commanding verse in the bible 1 John 2:17 (KJV) states," And the world passeth away, and the lust thereof: but he that doeth the will of God abideth forever." I desperately wanted to go to the kingdom of heaven when I died. Probably more than anyone alive right now considering I know for a fact heaven exists and God is real. I couldn't imagine the conversation I would have to endure with God if I died before carrying out his will. I was deeply conflicted. I was still no angel. And, as a result I would have to explain no book, no obedience, no holy walk, and no major change in my life. Therefore, I couldn't risk it another day. I literally locked myself in my room and wrote for hours! Previously, when I wrote short stories, screen plays, and poetry I would develop writer's block for days, weeks, or even months. But, as I began writing this book, things were different. My hands typed effortlessly and my thoughts flowed freely. I could literally feel the Holy Spirit take the wheel. On most days, I would write 25 to 30 pages in one day with ease. The words flowed so fluidly that I knew it was God! I felt it deep within my spirit as if the Holy Spirit moved within me to help me form the words on the page. The joy I experienced was insurmountable and I knew God was pleased. I was finally carrying out his will.

I sat in my room late one-night pondering. I placed my laptop to the side, took a break from writing, and reflected on how the Lord was truly a loving and forgiving God. I remembered how at times when I acted a fool, God was still faithfully by my side. Even when I didn't deserve it, he was there. I realize now that God is always aware of everything that we're going through. He's persistent and he's present. Nothing is new to our heavenly father. The Bible states in Job 28:24 (NIV), "For he views the ends of the earth and sees everything under the heavens." That means that God sees all, he knows all, and he watches all. Every single event that occurs in your life, God is aware it will happen. Every single person that you will encounter whether for a reason, a season or a lifetime, God has ordained it. We as human beings tend to be clueless to our daily interactions. We get lost in the daily minutiae of our lives like going to school, work, coming home, cooking, on social media, reading, gossiping, laughing, dating, spending time with family, friends, etc. We fail to focus on the significance of every single move that we make. It's key to realize that every decision that you make will impact your life. I had no clue that having an abortion in Detroit would cause me to die weeks later during Freshman Week in Atlanta. But, God knew! He knew it the first minute

Winston walked into Foot Action and spotted me at the register. He even knew when Winston gave me his phone number. Additionally, I had no clue in my haste to terminate a pregnancy that Dr. Sanjay would completely butcher my insides, I would still be pregnant, and experience a horrendous ectopic pregnancy in Atlanta. But, God knew! He even forewarned me when I heard the small voice at the abortion clinic say *"leave now"*. Yet, I didn't heed the warning. I didn't listen to the voice. Instead, I stayed on that hard cold table totally unaware of my fate. But, as traumatic as my entire near-death experience turned out to be, it was ordained and destined to happen. The reality is, had I not suffered through that horrendous ordeal, I would never have been blessed to transcend through the afterlife and have a near-death experience to hear the voice of God. I would have never turned my life around to stop my rebellious behavior and draw nearer to God. I would have never stopped questioning God's existence. I would have never had the experience necessary to write this book and share this testimony with you. God ordained every step in my life to bring me to this point. Just like he is ordering every step in your life to bring you to where you are today. God is truly incredible. He has a plan for me and please understand that he has a plan for you too!

I closed my laptop, leaned back on the bed, and reflected over my life. I realized there were so many times that God showered me with mercy, protection, and a legion of guardian angels to watch over me along the way. He always stood by my side even when I didn't know it nor expect it. I reflected on my near-death experience and the people that God placed in my life. I even pondered deeper to my wayward high school days in Detroit. I remembered many instances when my mother would fuss me out that I better not go to a party or club in a bad section of town. Needless to say, I would go anyway. I will never forget one time when I went with my older cousin, Tanya, to a club called The Dancery on Detroit's east side. It was a club known for many bad elements. But, it was also known as the "it" place to be amongst teens. Which in the whole scheme of things meant if it was popping I had to be there too. I shook my head as I closed my eyes and recalled the untimely events that took place that one dreadful night.

I made plans to head to the Dancery. But, I was upset that my sister didn't want to go. A few of my other friends faked out too. My only recourse was to drag my not-so-cool cousin Tanya along with me. She lacked serious style in the Fashionista department And, she didn't attend any social functions beyond family birthday parties to my knowledge. Matter of fact, my sister refused to hang out with her even though they were the same age. I only hoped she wouldn't act goofy and get us clowned, kicked out, or worse yet jumped in the club. The Dancery had a long history of many reckless endeavors and was known most notably for getting "shot up". However, even with its notorious reputation, it was surprisingly touted as the "it" place to be. All the cool kids hung out there. And since I considered myself cool, it only made sense for me to have my face in the place as well. I saw one of the popular kids from Cass Tech, Tone, hanging outside the club. He was caramel complexioned with a cute boyish face and bad boy persona. Tone was cool as a breeze and dressed to impress in a striped polo top and creased jeans. A signature gold chain hung lowly from his neck as he posted

I HEARD GOD'S VOICE

up against the wall with a diamond earring blinging from his ear.

"What's up Tone?" I coyly waved as I walked past.

"What up doe!" He grinned back.

A huge smile smeared across Tanya's face.

"Who is that?!" She grabbed my arm.

"Just a guy from school." I quickly filed in line.

I must've been really desperate to get out that night. I never went anywhere with my cousin Tanya. That might've been the primary reason I spoke to Tone. I needed to feel some cool vibes filter in from somewhere. I didn't hang with Tone or his crew at all. But, considering he was a card-carrying member of the in-crowd, that was definitely enough grounds for me to weave through formalities. While a lot of kids at Cass Tech assumed Tone sold drugs given his many lavish trinkets, I didn't know him well enough to dispel if the rumors were true. All I knew was I didn't live on the east side of Detroit. And, inside The Dancery, it was wise to have as many alliances as possible. You never knew when something would "pop off" literally and figuratively. Therefore, it was best to extend a friendly nod and a bit of pleasantries to as many people as possible. Tanya was ready to get her party on full throttle and quickly stepped ahead of me. She eased successfully past the security checkpoint and paid to go inside. I approached Security as three of Tone's friends rolled up. I thought they were a little underdressed to be at the club that night. But, unfazed by the well-dressed club goers, they casually walked up wearing black hoodies, blue jeans, and sneakers. They strolled around the metal railings and stopped alongside Tone and leaned against the wall as well. None of them went through the doors to gain entry into the club. They all simply posted on the wall and stared out at the parking lot as more patrons filtered through.

"You going in?" I quizzically asked Tone.

"Yeah, in a minute," He gazed out to the parking lot. "Ok, see you inside.

Security promptly frisked my legs and patted me down. I left Tone and his crew. I was too eager to get my party on as the loud vibrations from the hard bass beats lured me inside the club. I slowly strolled through the hallway and tried to locate my cousin who had already submerged deep on the scene. I told her in advance this was not the type of place to wander off. But, I guess she was too excited and fluttered on anyway. I peered inside the club trying to locate her. A fierce Jit battle was taking place front and center on the dance floor as two guys were giving serious footwork to fast techno beats. I leaned against the wall and stood on my tippy toes to get a better view. I turned momentarily to make sure I didn't step on anyone's sneakers. That was the epitome of antics that started many fights in the D. Luckily, tonight that wasn't the case. As I glanced over my shoulder, I saw Tone wildly staggering towards me. The awkwardness in his steps totally caught me off guard. He didn't seem drunk when I saw him a few minutes ago outside. He reached to grab the wall attempting to catch his balance.

"Tone, you ok?!" I quickly rushed towards him.

No sooner than I could ask. Tone collapsed right in front of me on the floor. Although it was dark inside the hallway, I immediately noticed his shirt was drenched in blood. I freaked!

"Somebody help!" I screamed. "He's been shot!"

Commotion erupted and pandemonium broke loose as people spilled inside the club; including two of Tone's other friends who were limping, leaning, and holding their sides clearly struck by bullets as well. Turns out, not too long after I walked inside the club, a car drove up and sprayed Tone and his crew. Had I not left when I did, I would've been victim to the drive-by shooting as well! That was the first clear indicator during my rebellious days that I realized God was faithfully by my side.

As I contemplated more and more about how God held me close, my mind soared to a time after my near-death experience that happened during my sophomore year of college. A college buddy of mine, Fontaine and I drove to Club Illusions in Atlanta. We were caught up in the moment and drinking beyond belief on the far southwest side of town, nowhere near campus, and totally wasted! It was 4:45 a.m. and I remembered thinking there was no way we were going to make it home. I drove an old 1986 Buick Century at the time. Everything was pretty much broken on that car; including cruise control. We were roughly 35 minutes from campus and I could barely keep my eyes open. I didn't know how I was going to drive all the way home. We didn't have enough money to get a hotel and there was no designated driver considering we were equally sloshed. So, I did the unthinkable. I did the one thing you should never do. I attempted to drive home totally drunk. We were headed down I-85 North towards downtown Atlanta. I was swerving beyond belief. My eyes were seriously heavy. I prayed very quickly to God "Please just let us make it home safely". My foot felt like lead and there was no way I could manage the speed limit consistently. A small voice inside of me said, "***Hit***

cruise control." I pressed the button. Magically, the cruise control button lit up on the dash, the system engaged, and the car began to cruise automatically at a steady pace. I managed to peer through slits of my eyelids and guided the vehicle home. By the grace of God, we made it to the dorm safely without injuring ourselves or anyone else. Needless to say, that was the only time the cruise control button worked in my car. It never worked since.

There's a saying that goes God watches over babies and fools. Too many times, my name fell in the fool pot. The above incidents were not the only encounters I experienced in haphazard situations. Fact about it is, I have entirely too many stories like the aforementioned ones to share. My junior year in college, I was cooking in the kitchen when a huge grease fire erupted. I panicked and was totally clueless how to handle the situation. So, what did I do? The one thing you should never do. I grabbed a huge pot of water and threw it on the flame! No one told me that this would make the fire worse. The flame totally erupted and blew up in my face. But, God is good! I stood there in only a white tank top and cheerleading shorts. Yet, I was not burned, scarred, or maimed. Even when the fire department came and noticed the charring which led all the way from the stove to the ceiling; I stood untouched. The point I'm trying to make is God had his hand on my life for a reason. He saved me time and time again when I was a teenager. He saved me time and time again as a young adult. And, he continues to save me, protect me, and bless me even till this day! I am far from perfect. Yet, our heavenly father continues to shine mercy upon me. Just like God has mercy on me, I also wrote this book to let you know that he has mercy on you. I am sure if you look back over your life, you too have a testimony to share. I'm sure you can pinpoint a situation that God saved you from and was faithfully by your side. Just know that God has a mission for your life and a purpose that you are destined to fulfill. He will keep you and protect you. He wants you to succeed! God wants you to just acknowledge him. He yearns for your love and your faithfulness. Once you submit your life to him, you will see a brand new awakening within your spirit. Your eyes will open and your circumstances will change.

TESTIMONY

I feel extremely honored to share my testimony with you today. Prior to dying and even after being resuscitated back to life, the question that burned deep inside of me was, "Why am I alive? What am I supposed to do?" I'm sure you've asked yourself that very same question. You may have even wondered, "Is there a God?" That's why I mustered enough courage to come forward to erase any doubts that you may have. Yes, God is real! I really want you to realize that you are alive because God has a purpose for your life. You are here because there is something that God wants you to do on earth. There is a mission that only you can fulfill. God is straightforward in all that he does. He is not a God of confusion. And, he expects direct execution of his plan. God chose you for a reason. He knows every intricate part of your life that even the Bible says in Matthew 10:30 (NIV), "And even the very hairs of your head are all numbered." This means that God has the most intimate knowledge of you. He cares about you so much that even the areas you think are minuscule are important to him. Nothing is overlooked. He has a bona fide plan for you. You just have to dig deep in your spirit to tap into his will for your life. It's so important that you make this your main priority to bring full completion to your calling. You need to do this. You have to do this. When God speaks to your spirit it will be very clear. You won't have to second-guess it. You will know without a shadow of a doubt that it's him. God is straight to the point and he doesn't waste time. To this day, it amazes me when God spoke to me he didn't give a long-winded speech. He didn't chastise me. He didn't condemn me. No! God allowed me to die. He brought me through the channels of a supernatural realm just to halt me in my tracks and say four words, *"Follow me my daughter"*. That was it. But, that was profound. It is imperative that you grasp the directness of our heavenly father. You do not have to fit into a certain mode for him to deliver you. You do not have to be perfect. I was far from it. Matter of fact, I'm still far from it. I struggle every day to do the right thing and live right just like you. It's important to remember that you were born into a world of sin. You were created a flawed being. But, God wants you to follow him and continuously grow along your spiritual walk to develop a nearness to him. He's waiting on you to take that step.

This world is so complex and moves at such a fast pace that we often get caught up in living that we fail to understand the simplicities of life. We fail to grasp how to live freely, to love freely, and to be free. I had to die to understand these simple and pure concepts. I am thankful that God spared my life and showered mercy upon me so that I was able to come back to life and share this good news with you. I realize now this was the purpose that God wanted me to fulfill. Now, it is time for you to dig deep within your spirit to connect to your purpose and grasp God's will for your life. It's important to align yourself with prayer partners, prayer warriors, and positive people in general. You need to seek out individuals in your circle that will help build you up, that will truly listen to you, and that will give you positive advice along the way. God placed a few prayer warriors in my life. I was blessed to be able to share my near-death experience with Rick. I felt safe disclosing this secret to him because I knew he wouldn't judge me. And, most importantly I knew he wouldn't call me crazy! That was one of the biggest fears in coming forward with my testimony. How do you tell someone that you died and heard the voice of God without them thinking that you're a bit loony? Rick was the exact opposite. He thought I was special and that my experience was supernatural. He even helped me to further understand and grasp what the word of God meant. For many years, I thought God was angry with me for not following him further through the black abyss when he said, "*Follow me my daughter*". I figured that was the reason my life was in such turmoil. But, Rick shared a different opinion. He said that maybe God meant for me to follow him in my daily walk on earth. God was aware of how disobedient that I had been, how doubtful I was, and how sacrilegious I was becoming. Therefore, God wanted to give me a second chance to get my soul right on earth and not be condemned to the pits of hell. So, he was simply instructing me to follow his ways. Those nuggets of wisdom that Rick shared made so much sense. I am grateful to him for giving me another perspective. And, I vowed to lead a closer walk with God.

But, the hardest thing I had to do before sharing my near-death experience with the masses, was disclosing it to my daughter. I knew if I published this book without sharing it with her first she would find out regardless. This was a tough pill to swallow. Parents want their children to view them in a perfect light. I was no different. But, this light of perfection creates a false shine that blinds our children's perception of us. And it can even cause feelings of inadequacy and imperfection as they try to live up to this false mode within themselves. I wasn't perfect. But, I didn't want my daughter to think that I was a failure either. So, here I found myself, once again, wrestling with this issue of transparency. It was challenging to share how I screwed up during my teenage years. It was difficult to reveal that I did shameful things that I later regretted. Somehow, I felt I would lose her respect if she knew my faults. I didn't want her to judge me as being weak. But, as God weighed in on my spirit, I decided it was critical to be more visible and real. I had to become more relatable and expose my truth especially if it meant a significant impact would be accomplished in saving her soul. I wanted my daughter to develop an intimate walk with God. And, I never wanted her to question God's existence. She needed to know the trauma that I endured to realize her birth was a miracle. No matter what anyone told her later in life, even if her friends questioned God's existence, I wanted her to affirm without a shadow of a doubt that God was tried, tested, and true. Plus, I wanted to prevent her from making the same mistakes that I made. It was paramount that she knew a wayward lifestyle would channel you to the pits of hell. So, in order to feed into her spirit, I shared with her so many exposing aspects about my life. I wanted her to grasp it was important to live your best life, carry out God's will, repent if you made mistakes, never give up, and try your best to stay on the right path. The road may not be easy, but with God on your side you can and you will make it.

This testimony was a long time coming. For the first time in my life, I feel like I'm truly free. But, this wasn't always the case. There are so many societal events that can harden the human heart. From police brutality, systemic racism, gender discrimination, age discrimination, and the list go on. At times, in my past, I found myself becoming engulfed with the perils of this world. I grew hardened. Slowly this same approach slipped into my religious views. America's history is so bitter in regards to race, we tend to place a person's skin color before the fortitude of their heart. This is a fact. The forefathers of the American Constitution were guilty of this act. They proclaimed black people were only considered three-quarters of a man. Yet, within the same constitution they claimed, "all men are created equal". Growing up in a country like America can skew your outlook on life. I found myself arguing the race of Jesus constantly for his existence to make sense to me. There are tens of thousands of illustrations where you see Jesus painted with long blonde hair and blue eyes. Yet, the Bible clearly states in Revelation 1:14-15 (KJV), "His head and his hairs were white like wool, as white as snow; and his eyes were as a flame of fire. And his feet like unto fine brass, as if they burned in a furnace." Plain as day, that description did not sound like white skin blue-eyed baby Jesus. I argued relentlessly that Jesus was black to anyone who would listen. My peers agreed. But, mainstream America adamantly did not. Therefore, I found hypocrisy in everything. Little did I know, as I waged this war, the devil was winning. At the end of the day, it didn't matter what color Jesus was. What mattered was Jesus existed. He had a mission to come and save the world from sin. Jesus was crucified so that our souls would be saved. However, at the time, this was not my focus. I needed to understand who Jesus was during my teen years. I reconciled if he wasn't black and if he didn't suffer as a black man, then I couldn't relate. You may hold a similar mantra. But, in the end, this point becomes fruitless. The interesting dynamic is this. As I literally died and heard the voice of God, I realized that race could not be placed inside a tiny box of reason. God has NO race. He's too powerful to even be categorized. That's the supreme race. Imagine that. God didn't sound "white". He didn't sound "black". His voice was as thunderous and powerful as anything I had ever heard. Yet, it was calm and loving at the same time. I am still mesmerized how his voice resonated from every angle and every direction. I felt fearful and shameful in his presence. That's how colossal God is. Before I died, I was arrogant, unabashed, and outspoken. Yet, in my death, I fell silent and did not utter one word. God had mercy on me and he literally blessed me with his words in my darkest hour. I am grateful that God chose me to bring this message to you. He knew it was paramount that I heard his voice as bona fide proof so that I would no longer deny his existence. God wanted me to experience resurrection from death to share an incredible testimony with you that he is powerful, wondrous, and alive. God is astonishing! He is amazing. And, God is still in the business of performing miracles. He is also capable of causing supernatural wonders in your life as well!

I realized shortly after my near-death experience that I was completely focused on all the wrong things. This prevented me from building a closer relationship with God. If you are honest with yourself, you will see, that you too are focused on the wrong things as well. It is important to overcome distracting obstacles in your life to focus on the fact that God is all that you need. He loves you unconditionally and he wants you to build a closer connection to him. But, you have to be ready. You have to be willing to go that extra mile and build that relationship with him.

There is so much turmoil in the world that at times it can appear the Devil is winning. But, the Devil is playing Jedi mind tricks to create confusion, hopelessness, and despair. Therefore, you must realize without a shadow of a doubt that God is **always** in control. The battle is not over even when the fight seems too big to win. The reality is with God all things are possible and with him you cannot fail. You just have to stay the course, be patient, humble, and believe God is working everything out in your favor. I pray that you are given solace as you read this book. It is my sincerest prayer that God will deliver and inspire you along your journey. If you are searching for salvation, I hope that it wraps its loving arms around you. If you are seeking redemption, I pray the mercy of God rains a fresh covering over your body so pure that you feel brand new inside and out. It is my honest prayer that you find contentment in your soul and that you are completely at peace. If you are struggling with a major issue, I want you to understand that God is already aware. Please realize that God is keeping you from falling for a reason. You have a higher calling to fulfill. The Lord has a mission that you must accomplish. It doesn't matter how many times you fall or fail. You must get up every time, shake yourself off, and try again. It doesn't matter how many people used you, abused you, or lied to you. You are worthy. You are a fighter. You are an overcomer. You are rich in spirit, resilience, and strength. Your story is just beginning; it is not over! If you are suffering from heartache, know this, you will survive. I know a person that you loved promised to love you forever. But, they left you. Yes, it hurts. But, guess what? That's not the person God wanted you to be with anyway. Be happy he or she left now. Be grateful you didn't waste another year, two years, or ten years dealing with the nonsense and lies. Rejoice in the fact that it's over and you can get on to living your best life! Now is the time that you stand tall, stand proud, and love yourself knowing that God loved you first. Go get your blessing. Don't wait another minute.

If you're reading this book and feel you're in a bad place without a clue how to make it through, get this, God knows how you will make it. Matter of fact, you are already surviving. You're not dead. And, guess what? God won't let you die. He's revealing to you just how strong you are. Rest assured you are going to come out on top. You may not know how. But, you didn't know how you were going to make it last year. But, you did. And, you will make it this year too! Get on your knees and thank God in advance for the glorious blessings he has for you. Your day is coming. You just have to be ready. Always remember the storm does not last always. Daylight must come in the morning. It's a natural fact. And, it's a brand new day.

I am so happy that I have finally reached a place in my life that I can speak these things to you. Trust and believe I've been there. I've battled with depression, student loans, single parenthood, unemployment, homelessness, lying lovers, false friends, and too much month at the end of my money! I've been there. But, I always had solace in knowing that there IS a God! I heard him. He delivered me. And, he will not let me fall or fail. Sure, he may let me go through the wringer for a while. But, it's only just a little while. The pain and turmoil will not last my entire life. And, it won't last your entire life either. Oftentimes, the situations that you find yourself in are based on bad decisions that you made. What's crazy is, it can be the smallest thing that you said, agreed to, or implicated. And, you find yourself still paying the price some five, ten, or twenty years later. Just know there's a lesson to be learned in those moments. You have to remain strong and know your breakthrough is coming. Some times in life, you find yourself the victim of circumstance. In those situations, I believe God is using you as an example. He wants his glory to shine through in your testimony. I also believe in moments like that, your blessing will be double and triple fold. Just stand firm. Stay prayed up and never let up. The enemy wants you to stop praying. He wants you to stop believing. And, he wants you to give up. I've learned that I get my biggest blessing when I'm praying and giving God the glory especially when all hell is breaking loose around me. That's when I praise God the hardest. It confuses the enemy. The enemy is thinking why is she smiling and praising while she's suffering? I praise even harder in my conflicting times because I know there is a huge blessing right around the corner if I can only stand firm and see it through. Every time, I'm right. I just keep trusting and believing. I challenge you to do the same and watch God work miracles in your life.

Life is so unpredictable. But, I would like to encourage you to never give up. I get solace in knowing that God is consistent and he's always on our side. Isaiah 54:17 (KJV) says, "No weapon that is formed against thee shall prosper." That means with God you have the victory! There is nothing that anyone can do to you that will destroy you. It just won't happen. Walk in triumph knowing and believing that God cannot and will not fail! Your day is coming and you will succeed. As you continue on your journey, walk with your head held high. Let your inner light shine. And, never be afraid to testify about the goodness of the Lord or the many blessings he's placed in your life. Always look for the silver lining in everything. Even when you think your situation is hopeless, just remember that someone else has it much worse than you. Remember to encourage those around you who are discouraged. Be that listening ear. Be that beacon of hope. And, always be a blessing to someone else. You have your very own experience, testimony, and story to share. While you may not have heard God's voice, you do have a special gift or talent that was specifically given to you. The Bible says in Romans 12:6 (KJV), "Having then gifts differing according to the grace that is given us." That makes you unique. No one was given the same gift that God gave you. It is yours to keep and no one can take it away. Be comforted that Jesus loved you enough that he made you special. Your gift is special. You are ordained to walk this earth and utilize your gift to help others. So you must gather the courage to do it.

I thank you for purchasing my book. I hope it touches your life immensely and strengthens your spirit to the core. Whenever you are discouraged I encourage you to pick up the Bible and submerse yourself deep in the word of God. It never lies. God is so omnipotent and powerful that he can never lie nor fail. I pray that whatever circumstance has a stronghold over your life that it will cease. I want you to receive all of the peace, joy, love, and happiness that you deserve. It is my wish that after reading this book you walk away with a renewed spirit and a greater expectation. I hope that you are immensely blessed.

As this book draws to a close, I ask that you link arms with me to say a prayer together to prepare you to step into your destiny:

"Father God, I thank you right now for continuously blessing me. I know that I have sinned and fallen short in your sight. I ask that you forgive me for my sins. I ask that you make me a better person today than I was yesterday. I ask that you strengthen and cover me in the armor of God to withstand the enemy. I know that the enemy comes to steal, kill, and destroy. I pray that you protect me. I pray that you protect my family, my friends, and my loved ones. Lord, I thank you for your son, Jesus! I thank you for him dying on the cross that I may be saved. Father, I thank you for the many people who have prayed for me. I thank you for my guardian angels that protect me every day. Please bless them as they continue to protect me. God, I know that you have a mission and a purpose for my life. I pray for clarity. I pray that you strengthen my inner spirit and discernment so that I may learn what that purpose is. I pray that when my foot slips off the path that you set before me, that you please help me quickly find my way so that I will not stray from you too long. I thank you in advance for the many blessings that you have in store for me. Thank you for never leaving me or forsaking me. Father, I pray that thy will be done! I not only ask for a major blessing in my life, but, I also pray that you help me to be a blessing to someone else. In, Jesus' precious name, I pray. Amen."

Watch miraculous things begin to shift in your life. When it happens, share, and be that living testimony! Now that you've claimed the victory, go forward and walk in the light. Live in the light. And, be the light that you are!

ABOUT THE AUTHOR

T. Marie Bell is an author, writer, public speaker, consultant, and mother. She has written several articles, blogs, books, and conducts writing workshops to help others hone their craft.

Ms. Bell enjoys playing the piano, swimming, cycling, volunteering, and traveling to exotic locations when possible. Currently, she resides in Atlanta, Georgia where she is working on her next book.

T. Marie loves connecting with readers! Please be sure to visit her website to stay up to date on the latest information regarding upcoming book projects, book signings, and more at: www.tmariebell.com

To contact T. Marie Bell for speaking engagements email her at: tmarie@tmariebell.com

---TO ORDER----

I Heard God's Voice

How I Died, Came Face-to Face with God, and Lived to Tell the Story

By: T. Marie Bell

If unavailable at your favorite bookstore, Success Write Now will fill your online order within 24 hours. Mail in orders take 5-7 business days to be delivered.
Email questions to: info@successwritenow.com

----Postal Orders----

Success Write Now
P.O. Box 55202
Atlanta, GA 30308

I Heard God's Voice
USA: $15.00 + $5 postage
Canada: $18.00 + $7 postage
Email to request bulk shipping price/discounts

Send _____ copies of *I Heard God's Voice* $_____

Shipping:$_____

Amount of Sale:$_____

Mail to:

Name: _____

Address:_____

City, State, Zip:_____

Cashier's Check enclosed:_____

Credit Card # _____

Expiration: _____ 3 Digit Code: _____

Made in the USA
Coppell, TX
22 November 2020

41881193R00098